BUREAUCRATIC POLITICS
AND
REGULATORY REFORM

Recent Titles in
Contributions in Political Science
Series Editor: Bernard K. Johnpoll

BUREAUCRATIC POLITICS
AND
REGULATORY REFORM

The EPA and Emissions Trading

BRIAN J. COOK

CONTRIBUTIONS IN POLITICAL SCIENCE, NUMBER 196

GREENWOOD PRESS

New York • Westport, Connecticut • London

Library of Congress Cataloging-in-Publication Data

Cook, Brian J., 1954–
  Bureaucratic politics and regulatory reform.

  (Contributions in political science,
ISSN 0147-1066 ; no. 196)
  Bibliography: p.
  Includes index.
  1. Air—Pollution—Law and legislation—United
States. 2. Administrative procedure—United States.
3. United States. Environmental Protection Agency.
I. Title. II. Series.
KF3812.C66   1988   344.73'046342   87-15032
                          347.30446342
  ISBN 0-313-25493-1 (lib. bdg. : alk. paper)

British Library Cataloguing in Publication Data is available.

Library of Congress Catalog Card Number: 87-15032
ISBN: 0-313-25493-1
ISSN: 0147-1066

First published in 1988

Greenwood Press, Inc.
88 Post Road West, Westport, Connecticut 06881

Printed in the United States of America

The paper used in this book complies with the
Permanent Paper Standard issued by the National
Information Standards Organization (Z39.48-1984).

10 9 8 7 6 5 4 3 2 1

To Ruth

CONTENTS

PREFACE

An important theme in modern American political thought, evident in much of the public discourse of the past 20 years, expresses a profound concern about the size of government, especially the national government, and also about the extent of government intrusion into the lives of individual citizens. Those most deeply worried about these issues perceive substantial dangers to such vital constituents of the public weal as sustained economic growth and freedom of individual choice as the core problems toward which scholarly study and concrete action must be directed. A certain irony attends this theme, because government itself must be enjoined to tame the excesses of the positive state.

One dimension of the growth and intrusiveness of the state is seen by many as the epitome of problems posed by large central governments. That dimension is of course regulation, which has become the target of considerable scholarly analysis and tangible political action aimed at shrinking the heavy-handed presence of government in a broad spectrum of social and economic activities. Often, the scholarly work has directly supported concrete proposals for change. Over the past 15 years, the increasing focus on regulation as the most egregious transgression of big government has blossomed into a loosely knit political movement aiming to transform the basic structure and function of regulation in the United States.

The movement for reform has directed much of its energy toward deregulation in traditional areas of economic regulation. The actions policy makers have taken to deregulate commercial airline services, interstate trucking, and banking are premiere examples. Reformers have also focused attention on environmental quality, workplace health and safety, and consumer protection laws, the so-called new social regulation. Here, however, scholarly analysis and public discourse have been noticeably unbalanced.

Much of the discussion about the new social regulation, as well as the alternatives to regulation, is conducted at the macro level. One finds little discussion of the

practical details of the activities and tasks performed by the regulators, their interactions with private sector organizations, or the behavior of their counterparts in
the private sector. If one of the fundamental problems with the new social regulation
is with its means and not its ends, what is needed is careful, empirically based
institutional and organizational analysis and design. (Graymer and Thompson 1982:
15)

This study is a modest attempt to heed this admonition and correct some
of the imbalance in research on social regulation.

The U.S. Environmental Protection Agency (EPA) is in many ways the
cornerstone of the administrative edifice of the new social regulation. The
agency has been the target of numerous efforts at regulatory reform, and
it is one of the few, if not the only, regulatory agency to implement programs that embody reformist ideas. The agency thus provides an appropriate target for empirically based organizational analysis of social
regulation, and emissions trading, the agency's premier reform program,
is central to the analysis in this study.

Using interviews with key agency decision makers and a host of interested
outside observers and analysis of the public record, I attempt to trace
through the formulation, legitimation, and implementation stages of the
policy process the debates over alternative forms of regulation advocated
by the movement for reform of social regulation. The focus is on air pollution control, and I examine policy and program decisions made both in
Congress and in the EPA. My central concern, however, is to gain some
understanding of the impact the movement for regulatory reform has had
on the EPA and, in turn, what effect internal characteristics of the agency
and its personnel have had on the prospects for success of the reform movement.

The nature of my research is necessarily provisional and exploratory.
Nevertheless, I believe it represents more than a mere addition to the long
list of both theoretical and assertive works on decision making in the formulation and implementation of public policy approached from an organizational point of view. Because this is a work of empirical research,
examining decisions documented in the public record and sifting through
the recollections of participants and observers involved in the process of
designing and implementing an important regulatory program, it provides
data not only on the issues debated by the parties involved, but also on the
factors that influenced the choices they made. I also attempt to provide some
admittedly quite speculative guidance on organizational change and policy
reform to individuals with a keen scholarly or practical interest in such
areas.

A note about my use of direct quotations from interviews is in order. I
have withheld the names of the individuals whose comments I have employed extensively throughout the book. I found that having the decision

makers involved in this case of regulatory reform politics express themselves in their own words drove home the points I sought to emphasize much more forcefully than paraphrasing their observations could have done. In exchange for the privilege of using their words directly, I readily agreed to protect the confidentiality of my sources.

I have accumulated a great many debts in the course of completing this book. My intellectual debts are especially great. Whatever contributions to scholarship and knowledge this book makes would not have been possible without the strong intellectual foundations provided by my principal task masters in graduate school at the University of Maryland, Steve Elkin and Joe Oppenheimer. Clarence Stone, Ric Uslaner, and Wallace Oates also provided much helpful guidance and many useful criticisms. A special measure of thanks must also go to Rich Liroff of the Conservation Foundation, who spent many hours discussing regulatory reform and emissions trading with me, and guided me through many of the intricacies of air pollution regulation. I would in addition like to thank Paul Quirk, who suggested one or two strategically important changes to the manuscript.

I owe a special debt of gratitude to John Palmisano, who while still at EPA enthusiastically embraced my research project from the start. He pointed me in the right direction toward people to talk to and documents to examine. He was especially generous of his time and good humor. Thanks also to Ivan Tether of EPA for his help and guidance in making contacts with the right people and obtaining the hard data I needed. Most important, my sincerest appreciation to all the individuals who were so generous of their time and attention as they endured interviews with me. I was most impressed with their patience and their professionalism. None of this would have been possible without their cooperation.

I would like to acknowledge the generous support for my research provided by the National Science Foundation under grant SES–83–15049. Many, many thanks must also go to Terry Reynolds and the word processing staff at Clark University for their help in preparing the manuscript.

Finally, I save my greatest expression of love and gratitude for my family, who gave me emotional sustenance and expressed confidence in my abilities to complete the project when I had my doubts. I hope this final product is worthy of their expectations.

Of course, no one mentioned above bears any responsibility for the errors that will surely be found in these pages. For those I am fully accountable.

ABBREVIATIONS

AQCR	Air Quality Control Region
BACT	Best Available Control Technology
CAB	Civil Aeronautics Board
CARB	California Air Resources Board
CBE	Citizens for a Better Environment
CEA	Council of Economic Advisors
CEQ	Council on Environmental Quality
CFC	Chlorofluorocarbon
COWPS	Council on Wage and Price Stability
DCRG	Domestic Council Review Group
EPA	Environmental Protection Agency
ERC	Emission Reduction Credit
ETPS	Emissions Trading Policy Statement
HUD	Housing and Urban Development
ICC	Interstate Commerce Commission
JEC	Joint Economic Committee
LAER	Lowest Achievable Emission Rate
NAAQS	National Ambient Air Quality Standards
NHTSA	National Highway Traffic Safety Administration
NRDC	Natural Resources Defense Council
NSPS	New Source Performance Standards
OIRA	Office of Information and Regulatory Affairs
OMB	Office of Management and Budget
OPM	Office of Planning and Management

OSHA   Occupational Safety and Health Administration
PPBS   Planning-Programming-Budgeting System
PSD   Prevention of Significant Deterioration
RACT   Reasonably Available Control Technology
RARG   Regulatory Analysis Review Group
RRS   Regulatory Reform Staff
SIP   State Implementation Plan
SOHIO   Standard Oil of Ohio
TDP   Tradable Discharge Permit
UARG   Utility Air Regulatory Group
VOC   Volatile Organic Compound

BUREAUCRATIC POLITICS
AND
REGULATORY REFORM

1

THE REGULATORY REFORM LANDSCAPE

Petition for a redress of grievances provoked by government regulation is not a new phenomenon. Neither is the development of a loosely organized and politically influential movement for regulatory reform. Calls for political leaders to do something about the problems engendered by regulation have been heard for as long as the federal government has actively and systematically intervened in private economic activity. Yet the grand crescendo of voices raised in support of reform, resonating across the 1970's and into the 1980's, is noteworthy for its broad-based public support, and thus its political potency, for its reach across the ideological spectrum, counting well-known liberals, moderates, and conservatives (including four presidents) among its members, and for the dedication and commitment shown by its most persistent warriors.

This latest incarnation of the broadly based effort to gain control of, and to change substantively the direction of, government regulatory activity reached its pinnacle with Ronald Reagan's 1980 presidential candidacy and election. Pledging to do something to curb the excesses of the positive state, especially the seemingly unquenchable thirst of the federal government to intrude into people's private business, President Reagan's agenda included the outline of a program for "regulatory relief" that had some appeal for regulatory reformers of all stripes.[1]

Unfortunately for many in the legion of reformers, the uneasy consensus that congealed around President Reagan's vague pronouncements about regulation has come unravelled.[2] Deregulation is under increasingly sharp attack. In the face of mounting failures of banks and savings and loans, and the growing economic concentration in commercial air passenger service, many of the successes of deregulation are now regarded as excesses. Reform of social regulation has been stymied, despite the achievements of reform-minded administrators recounted in this book. Among the other obstacles to further reform, critics have charged that President Reagan's designs for regulatory relief have meant retreating from the basic goals of much social regulation, goals toward which the public continues to be strongly committed.

What has happened to regulation, to regulators, and to the agencies they inhabit during the "Reagan era" is grist for the mills of other analysts (see Eads and Fix 1984; Seidman and Gilmour 1986: chapter 6). The story that follows is about decisions that were made and actions that were taken when the movement for regulatory reform was still vigorous and building momentum.

At the center of both the wave of "new" social regulation that arose in the late 1960's and early 1970's and the subsequent efforts to gain better control over this massive federal endeavor to protect people's health and safety stands the U.S. Environmental Protection Agency (EPA). Established late in 1970 as the federal government's concrete response to widespread public demands for a cleaner, more healthful environment, the EPA quickly became the most visible symbol of the extended struggle to reduce the hidden dangers in America's food, water, air, medicine, workplaces, and living spaces. The EPA thus also became the principal target of attempts to tone down the overzealousness and blatant paternalism many saw in this unbridled burst of government regulatory activity.

Almost since the agency's inception, attempts at influencing the procedures and outcomes of the regulatory decision process in the federal government generally, wrapped in the cloak of reform, have been aimed specifically at the EPA. The most recent version of regulatory reform to permeate the agency has concentrated on changing the techniques EPA and state regulators use to control air pollution from stationary sources. A series of reform initiatives and incremental program changes, grouped together under the current label of "emissions trading," developed largely during the Carter administration. The implementation of these reforms has carried over into the Reagan years, and this attempt at reform of environmental regulation has had a profound effect on how the agency goes about its business. To fully understand the nature of this reform effort, however, some preliminary landscaping is necessary.

ORGANIZATION OF THE BOOK

This book is about the collision of the movement for regulatory reform with the internal politics of an important administrative agency. The drive for regulatory reform that rose to prominence in the 1970's and pushed on into the 1980's had a significant and lasting influence on public policy in this country, affecting the lives of virtually every citizen. While scholars have dissected the anatomy of this reform movement and its impacts extensively, they have been less attentive to the influence this reform movement has had on individual regulatory agencies, and to the fate of the movement within any given agency. This study of the Environmental Protection Agency and its principal regulatory reform program, emissions trading, represents a modest attempt to further the understanding of scholars and practitioners on this important topic.

In the remainder of this introductory chapter I attempt to fill in those parts of the broad canvass of regulatory reform pertinent to understanding the interaction of bureaucratic politics and reform politics that took place inside the EPA in connection with the development and implementation of emissions trading. In particular, this introduction makes some distinctions between various kinds of regulation and between various kinds of reformist remedies for the problems of regulation. The chapter then summarizes the history of administrative reforms aimed at social regulation, of which the most recent reforms in the EPA are a part. The chapter also raises those research questions that seem most relevant to understanding the intermingling of bureaucratic politics and regulatory reform in the agency. Chapter 2 provides additional background material by summarizing the controversy concerning regulatory form, including brief descriptions of the regulatory alternatives reformers have advocated, and the principal arguments in the debate over those alternatives.

In chapter 3 I trace the legislative context within which emissions trading developed in the EPA. Using congressional documents and interviews with congressional staff, I reconstruct the history of congressional attention to the potential use of economic incentives in pollution control. The evidence shows that although Congress gave arguments favoring the use of economic incentives in pollution control due consideration, it never had any intention of endorsing such regulatory alternatives in any effective form. The evidence also leads me to question the extant scholarly explanations for the reluctance of Congress to accept incentive-based regulatory schemes for pollution control, and to offer the outline of an alternative explanation.

Chapter 4 is a detailed chronicle of the development of emissions trading, and thus of the larger movement for regulatory reform in the EPA. I emphasize the interaction between the policy intentions of the reform movement and the organizational character of the agency. Hence I consider not only the policy changes wrought by the drive for reform, but the organizational and staffing changes that occurred as well, arguing that these latter changes were the key to the policy change strategy of the EPA reformers. The chronicle brings to light basic information not only regarding the impact the movement for regulatory reform had inside the EPA, but also regarding how the fundamental organizational characteristics of the EPA shaped the direction reform took within the agency.

The next two chapters explore the controversies generated by the regulatory reform effort in the EPA as embodied in emissions trading. Chapter 5 examines the implementation problems emissions trading has faced. The chapter reviews the various conflicts that have raged in the EPA and the surrounding environmental policy community over the feasibility of the emissions trading program and the regulatory techniques the program uses. I argue in chapter 6, however, that the contentiousness surrounding emissions trading was less about disagreements over technique and much more about fundamental philosophical conflicts concerning the design of administrative structures to achieve broad public policy goals. Inside the EPA, these philosophical conflicts can be traced at least partly to contrasting professional ideologies among EPA staff.

In chapter 7 I return to the theme of organizational ethos or character to complete the story of the interaction between bureaucratic politics and regulatory reform in the EPA. I then explore the relationship between organizational character and policy reform in more general terms. I consider the prospects for regulatory reform in the future given the influence regulatory agencies can exert on the direction reform may take. I also pursue the issue of political leadership in public organizations, arguing that if my EPA case study indicates anything, it is that political executives can exert important influence over the direction of policy within a bureaucratic agency. Such a conclusion is contrary, perhaps, to the weight of the evidence on this question. The chapter and the book conclude with some speculative discussion about the practical role of policy analysis in administrative policy making, about the nature of policy reform and organizational change in a bureaucracy, and about what the politics of regulatory reform suggest about the central role ideas play in driving the policy process.

WHAT KIND OF REGULATION?

Most studies of regulation and attempts at its reform now take special care to distinguish between two principal categories of regulation.[3] The first category, variously labeled as "early," or "old style," "economic" regulation, represents attempts by the federal government (and often the states as well) to control prices, entry, exit, and conditions of service in specific industries or economic activities, which, according to many of the statutes granting federal agencies the power to regulate, are "affected with the public interest." In addition to the efforts by the government embodied in economic regulation primarily to correct or offset the problems created by monopoly practices in a free-market economy, the federal government also has engaged in fostering monopolies or cartels to encourage certain new kinds of economic activity. Policy makers have regarded national monopolies for some kinds of economic activities, especially public utilities, such as the generation of electricity, the distribution of natural gas, and waterway development and flood control, as necessities. Nonetheless, being monopolies, policy makers have insisted that these activities be regulated.

"New," or "new style," "social" regulation, on the other hand, is principally concerned with the achievement of broad social goals with respect to safety, health, employment fairness, and related issues. Although social regulation dates back to nineteenth-century efforts to limit water pollution discharges and turn-of-the-century attempts to clean up the wretched conditions associated with meat packing and other forms of food processing, most social regulation originated in the 1960's and 1970's wave of federal legislation focusing on environmental quality, worker health and safety, product quality and safety, and equal opportunity in housing and employment.

Other distinctions between economic and social regulation are also important. Whereas economic regulation is largely aimed at specific industries or economic sectors (for example, transportation, banking, merchant shipping), most kinds of social regulation encompass broad classes of industry and cut across economic sectors. For example, air and water pollution control laws concern all types of industries, as do workplace health and safety regulations and consumer protection rules. Further, the organizations that develop and administer the rules and regulations differ between the two broad categories of regulation. Economic regulation is administered by so-called independent commissions, independent in the sense that overhead political control by the president and Congress is somewhat circumscribed. Social regulation is administered by executive branch agencies, either within cabinet departments (for example, the Occupational Safety and Health Administration [OSHA] in the Labor Department), or separate from them (for example, the EPA). These agencies tend to be under much tighter presidential, and congressional, control.[4]

Social and economic regulation may also be distinguished by the differences in the approach to regulation they exhibit. Economic regulation has often been undertaken at the request of an industry, often for purposes of protecting that industry from competition. Social regulation is rarely demanded by industry. Usually such regulation is forced on industry by Congress responding to the demands of nonindustry groups. Finally, one may distinguish the two kinds of regulation by the justifications offered to promote them. Economists, for example, now have abandoned most of the original justifications for economic regulation, such as the threat of monopoly or oligopoly, or the threat of suboptimal income distribution from unregulated industries. Economic regulation currently has few clear justifications and few friends (see, for example, White 1981: 28–31). Social regulation continues to be justified, even by many economists, because the social goals sought by this type of regulation cannot, it is argued, be achieved even by a perfectly functioning market. The problems engendered by externalities and public goods, generally placed under the rubric of "market failure," require some collective, that is, governmental, response to achieve broad public objectives (White 1981: 34; Eads and Fix 1984: 14).

WHAT KINDS OF REMEDIES?

Regulatory reform, in its broadest, most ambiguous sense, means doing something to change the regulatory status quo. This may include everything from expanding regulatory programs to dismantling regulatory regimes altogether. In a somewhat more restrictive sense, and in the most familiar use of the term, regulatory reform means doing something to prune back government regulation and gain control over regulatory agencies and regulatory decision processes. Regulatory reformers have proffered a wide variety of remedies for "overregulation" under the rubric of reform. The remedies can be organized and classified in a number of ways.

Kenneth Meier's (1985: 284–299) typology places reform proposals into one of two categories. Where regulation in general is seen as the problem, the solution is less regulation. Where regulation is seen as necessary, but the pattern of regulation has proved to be ineffective, the solutions are either to decentralize decision making, through the use of market-oriented mechanisms, or to centralize decision making in the political branches of the federal government, wresting some control of policy making away from unelected, and therefore potentially unresponsive, bureaucrats. Under market-oriented reforms Meier includes antitrust action, general deregulation, cost-benefit analysis, incentive systems, and nontax incentives. Under responsiveness reforms Meier includes actions to make regulations, and regulators, more responsive to consumers, to the president, to Congress, and to the courts.

Alan Stone (1982: 237–239) distinguishes between "old reform" and "new reform." Stone describes old reform as including remedies that seek ways to curb delay and red tape in the regulatory process, and the establishment of other procedural reforms. Stone characterizes new reform as seeking substantive changes in regulation, especially by comparing extant regulatory structures with other alternatives, particularly the market.

Stone (1982: 246–249) goes on to categorize regulatory reformers. The "traditionalists" he identifies are concerned with the abuse of economic power. They regard regulation as better than the market in many instances. Traditionalists focus their remedies on the continuing need to improve the regulatory process. Stone's "restrictivists" hold a strong distaste for government intervention and control of the economy, although they concede the need for some regulation. Restrictivist prescriptions include a return to the market wherever possible, the substitution of incentives and property rights mechanisms for direct regulation, and the use of cost-benefit and cost-effectiveness analysis in regulatory decision making. Finally, Stone describes a category of reformers he calls "populists," who regard regulation as acceptable when it operates in pursuit of socially acceptable goals. Populists reject regulation when it aids corporate, rather than consumer, interests. Populists advocate procedural and organizational reforms, especially

increasing public participation in regulatory decision making and the modification of agency proceedings to allow greater public involvement.

The analysis provided by Eads and Fix (1984: 88–89, 95–104) is also useful
for sifting through the profusion of remedies aimed at the problems associated with regulation. Like Stone, Eads and Fix categorize remedies according to the types of individuals and groups who advocate them.
Libertarians, in the Eads-Fix typology, generally advocate dispensing with
social regulation altogether. A second group, dominated by business, objects
not to the principle of social regulation, but to its volume. The group
advocates reducing the burdens of regulation through a variety of mechanisms, including expanded presidential oversight, the regulatory budget,
cost-benefit analysis, and the elimination of clearly unrealistic goals (for
example, the Federal Water Pollution Control Act's goal of zero discharge
into navigable waterways by 1985). The third group, consisting of economists and other policy analysts, supports social regulation as a cure for
market failure, but objects to the techniques being used to achieve the goals
espoused in much social regulation. This group advocates changing the way
regulation is structured, in particular, replacing command-and-control regulation with market-like systems.

In the face of this dizzying array of remedies and analyses of types of
remedies, it is important not to lose sight of the fundamental structure of
the regulatory process. As Charles Schultze (1977) argues, the regulatory
process is predicated on two distinct decisions. A decision-making body
must first decide to take regulatory action, that is, to intervene in and control
some social or economic activity. A second critical decision follows the
decision to intervene, and that is the choice of the means by which the
intervention will be carried out. As Schultze shows, policy makers have a
wide range of alternative regulatory means from which to choose. "Should
intervention be carried out by grafting a specific command-and-control
module—a regulatory apparatus—onto the system of incentive-oriented enterprise, or by modifying the informational flow, institutional structures,
or incentive pattern of that private system?" (Schultze 1977: 13)

Given the basic structure of the regulatory process, the distinction between economic and social regulation, and the tendency of reformers and
analysts to match certain kinds of remedies to one or the other major types
of regulation, I will use a more restrictive definition of the term regulatory
reform throughout this study, a definition that is essential for understanding
the story that is to follow. In general, the most drastic remedy, deregulation,
is aimed at reversing the fundamental decision to intervene in a social or
economic activity. Except for the early years of President Reagan's program
of regulatory relief (Eads and Fix 1984) deregulation as a remedy has been
reserved strictly for economic regulation, largely because such regulation
is no longer regarded as necessary (see Breyer 1982; Stone 1982: 250–251;
Derthick and Quirk 1985: 33–34). Regulatory reform, on the other hand,

is directed at modifying the choice of the means to be used to achieve intervention, that is, altering the *form* regulation is to take or changing the techniques regulators use. This version of regulatory reform is aimed specifically at social regulation, and the remedies are rooted in microeconomic theory. Stone's restrictivists and Eads and Fix's economists are thus the principal advocates of this kind of regulatory reform (also see White 1981: 35–43). Chapter 2 explores in greater detail the types of alternative techniques advocated in this version of regulatory reform and the principal arguments in the regulatory form debate.

Reform focused on the structure and techniques of social regulation is thus the kind of policy change, embodied in EPA's program of emissions trading, pushed by reformers inside the agency, whose exploits are retold in this study. A brief history of how this brand of regulatory reform came to the EPA accents some of the key external motifs that will become evident in what the EPA reformers did, and what resulted from their actions, as the story unfolds.

PRESIDENTIAL EFFORTS TO REFORM SOCIAL REGULATION

Martha Derthick and Paul Quirk observe that presidents have special concerns about economic efficiency.

Long the locus of institutionalized concerns about the efficiency of the federal government's own operations, the Executive Office of the President [has] also become the center of governmental concern about the efficiency of the economy as a whole, for which the president increasingly [bears] responsibility in his role as the economy's manager. (Derthick and Quirk 1985: 30)

LeRoy Graymer and Fredrick Thompson echo this argument, adding a normative slant, and link it directly to regulation.

To the extent the president is interested in reelection and the success of his party, he ought to be interested in promoting allocative efficiency through governmental action. . . . [T]he president has a political interest in promoting economic efficiency (and good macroeconomic performance) in general. Improving the efficiency and effectiveness of regulations and removing those that impose costs greater than the social benefits they provide can make an important contribution to the president's perceived need to improve the performance of the economy. (Graymer and Thompson 1982: 276–277)

The principal organizational homes for concerns about efficiency in the executive branch are the Council of Economic Advisors (CEA) and the Office of Management and Budget (OMB). Senior White House staff also have special concerns in this area expressly because the political fortunes of the president are now so closely linked to the performance of the nation's economy.

As the size of the social regulatory apparatus, and the activity it generated, expanded rapidly in the early 1970's, it alarmed key figures in the Nixon administration with special concerns about efficiency and the health of the economy, in particular Commerce Secretary Maurice Stans and OMB Director George Schultz. Schultz's unease focused in particular on the budgetary implications of EPA's rapidly expanding staff and program operations and the concomitant acceleration in resource demands. Stans worried about the costs to industry posed by the many new regulations issued by the agency and he was angered by the law suits EPA had brought against major industrial polluters. Stans and Schultz communicated their concerns to the White House, and subsequent actions culminated in the establishment of the first formal process for presidential staff review of, and control over, social regulatory policy accompanied by attempts to inject a greater concern for economic considerations into the decision making processes of social regulatory agencies.

The process was dubbed the "Quality of Life Review." It emphasized prior notice about major regulatory actions by an agency being sent to the White House and other key administrative units, and the opportunity for interagency comment. The Quality of Life Review committee, composed of the Domestic Council, headed by Presidential Advisor John Ehrlichman, and other members of the White House staff, oversaw the review process. Although ostensibly intended to provide early review and comment procedures for the actions of all social regulatory agencies, "in practice only EPA's rules were singled out for review under the Quality of Life Review procedures" (Eads and Fix 1984: 49).

The Commerce Department was frequently at the center of heated debates about proposed EPA regulations as a result of the Quality of Life Review. The White House staff often found itself in a mediating role. The recurring clashes between Commerce and EPA under the Quality of Life Review established a pattern that in later years would involve the Commerce Department in EPA reforms on a number of occasions, including the development of emissions trading (see chapter 4). Little additional input into the review process beyond that supplied by what were the principal organizations at the time (OMB, Commerce, EPA, and the White House) occurred, although the CEA and the Council on Environmental Quality (CEQ) participated sporadically.

The immediate impact of the Quality of Life Review and Commerce Department challenges to EPA regulations was to force EPA Administrator William Ruckleshaus to create a unit in the agency staffed by economists. Ruckleshaus intended this unit to produce information and analyses he could use to rebuff White House and Commerce Department attempts to preempt EPA's regulatory decisions. Thus was born EPA's Office of Planning and

Evaluation (later the Office of Planning and Management), which would come to serve as the organizational home for reformers in the agency (see Marcus 1980a: 289; Eads and Fix 1984: 49).

The Quality of Life Review process continued to operate as Richard Nixon resigned under the cloud of Watergate and Gerald Ford took control of the administration. President Ford's special economic concerns centered on inflation, and he took two key steps in his fight against the inflationary dragon that would prove critical in the progress of presidential efforts to reform social regulation.

First, President Ford issued Executive Order 11801, requiring the preparation of "inflation impact statements" for all major legislation and regulations proposed by executive branch agencies. The president's executive order also empowered the OMB to review all major legislative proposals, rules, and regulations issued by agencies for their inflationary impacts, with a special focus on the private economic costs of regulation. Second, the president sought from Congress, and received, legislation establishing a Council on Wage and Price Stability (COWPS), charged with monitoring inflation in the economy and dissuading industry and labor from making decisions that could have inflationary effects. Ford also assigned COWPS a role in monitoring the inflationary effects of government actions.

OMB and COWPS thus shared inflation monitoring authority, but the actions of COWPS staff soon led to the bulk of any regulatory review work related to that monitoring being undertaken by COWPS. The Government Programs and Regulations division in COWPS, unaware of the Quality of Life Review process, sought to use its inflation monitoring power to pressure executive branch agencies into analyzing the likely economic consequences of regulations the agencies proposed. The division went even farther by initiating a program of public filings, preparing analyses of the economic impact of proposed rules and regulations and filing them on the public record of agencies proposing new rules. The COWPS filings soon evolved into quite formal economic analyses of proposed regulations, filed at the end of the public comment period for an agency's notice of proposed rule making published in the *Federal Register*. Eads and Fix (1984: 52) note that COWPS made approximately 125 such filings by the end of the Ford administration.

Other innovations in regulatory oversight occurred during Gerald Ford's tenure in office. A special task force called the Domestic Council Review Group (DCRG) on Regulatory Reform was established, which, among other actions, examined the Quality of Life Review process. DCRG noted the criticisms the process had encountered, especially from environmentalists, but judged the process to have been helpful to EPA. The Quality of Life Review Process had essentially withered away by then, however, having been supplanted by the more effective, and congressionally endorsed, practice of public filings by COWPS. In addition, regulatory oversight expanded beyond EPA to such agencies as OSHA and the National Highway Traffic Safety Administration (NHTSA). Eads and Fix (1984: 53) also argue that the oversight process exhibited increased professionalism and institutionalization. Finally, the notion that the basic goals of social regulation were appropriate, but that the means used to pursue those goals should encompass the most efficient, least expensive techniques possible, began to percolate through the organizations responsible for presidential oversight of regulation.

With Gerald Ford's loss to Jimmy Carter in the 1976 election, presidential attempts to shape regulatory policy entered a new and more vigorous phase. President Carter gave the responsibility for developing a new regulatory review and control process, which would go beyond the procedures of the Ford administration, to his CEA chairman, Charles Schultze. The process devised by Schultze focused on expanding economic analyses of regulations beyond the narrow comparison of benefits and costs and toward the development of cost–effective regulations. Schultze's process also created formal interagency review procedures under the control of a newly formed Regulatory Analysis Review Group (RARG). RARG was chaired by CEA but staffed by COWPS. RARG members included representatives from the economic agencies (Treasury, Commerce, and OMB) and all executive branch agencies with significant regulatory responsibilities, EPA being the most conspicuous.

President Carter's approach to regulatory oversight and reform evolved along two tracks. With respect to economic regulation, the Carter administration strategy pursued deregulation through the support of both legislative and administrative initiatives, the best example being airline deregulation, pushed by Edward Kennedy (D-MA) in the Senate and Alfred Kahn as chairmen of the Civil Aeronautics Board (CAB). For social regulation, the Carter administration first sought to manage regulatory activity in a more effective and efficient manner. Second, and more important for the story that is to follow, the Carter social regulatory reform strategy encouraged the development of innovative regulatory techniques and new ways to regulate. This latter dimension of the regulatory reform strategy led, first, to Executive Order 12044, issued by President Carter in the spring of 1978. The order required all executive branch regulatory agencies to provide a regulatory analysis to accompany any major new proposed regulation, and emphasized that agencies should include in their analyses consideration of alternatives to the actual regulations chosen.

Second, a few months later Carter created the Regulatory Council and endorsed some minor procedural changes in the functions of the RARG. The Regulatory Council consisted of representatives from all executive branch agencies having significant regulatory responsibilities. The Regulatory Council was chaired by the EPA administrator and funded out of EPA's budget. Although it was seen as a counterweight to RARG and a "regulators lobby," the Regulatory Council became heavily involved in publicizing the problems of regulation and promoting innovative regulatory techniques. It sought to encourage member agencies to make use of newly devised regulatory concepts and tools.[5]

Carter's EPA administrator, Douglas Costle, took the work of the group he chaired quite seriously, appointing a key deputy strongly committed to environmental policy reform to head an expanded staff of economists and policy analysts, and giving that group increased leeway to pursue regulatory reform within the agency. The result was a program called "controlled trading" in the Carter EPA, and emissions trading in the Reagan EPA. The program is the end product of an extended sequence of decisions and actions that I trace beginning with chapter 3.

Chapter 4 picks up the story of presidential regulatory reform efforts and how they are played out in detail in the EPA through the middle of the second year of Ronald Reagan's term in office. It is therefore appropriate to explore more fully the rationale behind this study's focus on bureaucratic politics and regulatory form in the EPA.

THE RESEARCH OBJECTIVES

The fundamental questions this study seeks to answer are simple. First, what impact did the regulatory reform movement of the 1970's and 1980's, particularly in its days of vigor and growth during the Carter administration, have on a prominent regulatory agency? Second, how did the internal politics of that agency shape the direction the regulatory reform movement followed inside the agency? That very basic empirical research in case study form (see the appendix for a discussion of the research methodology) is necessary to begin to answer these questions reveals the divergent paths social science research has taken in the study of economic regulation and deregulation, on one side, and social regulation and regulatory reform, on the other.

One of the basic differences in the two research paths is that although research on both economic and social regulation has focused on policy questions, research on economic regulation has also focused on administrative organizations, while research on social regulation has tended to ignore them. The attention, in research on economic regulation and efforts to deregulate many service industries, given to the regulatory agencies involved stems from the "interest-capture" theory, developed first by political scientists and then independently by economists.[6]

Briefly, the interest-capture theory asserts that over time the interests of a regulated industry come to dominate the decisions and actions of the agency that is supposed to regulate the industry. The regulated interests manage to capture the regulators for a variety of reasons. The commission form of regulatory organization provides too little overhead political control by the political branches, thus affording the "independent" agencies little in the way of protection from the direct influence of powerful political and economic interests. Also, a revolving door frequently develops between the regulatory agency and the regulated interests, and personnel from regulated industries often become regulators, and vice versa. The result of the control regulated interests gain over their ostensible government masters, even if the objective of the authorizing legislation establishing the agency and the rules it issues is to provide some form of protection to a designated industry or economic activity, is a nearly impenetrable armor against competition that forms around the protected industry, to the clear detriment of economic efficiency. The presumed capture of regulatory agencies by regulated interests has provoked analysts and policy makers to attack such occurrences as the unconscionable private use of public resources.

With this theory in hand, the response of researchers has been to analyze regulatory agencies, both in terms of internal characteristics and external environment, especially the relationship with regulated parties, to discover if interest capture has occurred, to understand how it has occurred or might occur in the future, and perhaps to develop prescriptions on how to avoid it. The response of policy makers has been the consideration of fundamental changes in agency organization and mission, or, more drastically, the complete dismantling of agencies and programs.

In research on social regulation and regulatory reform, the relative absence of a focus on administrative organizations has a number of origins. One strong influence is that few agencies responsible for administering social regulation are organized on the commission model of regulatory administration. Although there are exceptions, as I have already noted most social regulatory agencies are more closely tied to the executive branch, either as independent agencies like EPA, or as bureaus in cabinet departments. The primary reason behind this basic difference in organizational type is that, as Ackerman and Hassler (1981) explain for the EPA, by the time many of the social regulatory agencies were created, Congress had already become sensitive to the weaknesses of the regulatory commission model and the threat of interest capture and sought to steer clear of those problems (see the expanded discussion of this topic in chapter 7).

Another strong influence behind the infrequent focus on agencies in research on the reform of social regulation stems from who is doing the research. As previously noted, political science has maintained a strong presence in the study of economic regulation and deregulation, and the character of the discipline has led it to focus on systemic and institutional concerns, such as the relationship between interest groups and administrative agencies. The theories of economists have led them to similar sets of concerns. Recently, political scientists have begun to question the entire basis of interest-capture theory (see Wilson 1980; Derthick and Quirk 1985; and the expanded discussion in chapter 7). Economists have thus come to dominate research on economic regulation and the need to deregulate that draws on interest-capture theory or related arguments.

In research and prescription regarding social regulation and its reform, economists have had the field largely to themselves. This has been the case because the policies have been seen as the principal source of trouble, not the agencies in charge of implementing those polices.[7] Because microeconomic theory and welfare economics easily lend themselves to the prescription of alternative policy instruments, and because political science does not have a similarly coherent theoretical framework amenable to a focus on programmatic concerns, economists are the most powerful force in research on the reform of social regulation. Political scientists who have done work in the area have worked largely within the microeconomic perspective, have offered pragmatically based correctives to the dearth of reality in some economists' prescriptions, or have sought to shed light on a set of philosophical concerns that fall outside the world view of most economists.

For these reasons and for others, research on social regulation and its reform has not given much attention to the organizations involved. Yet research on the reform of social regulation has focused on the central issue of regulatory form and debates have arisen about the viability of various alternative techniques and structures for social regulation. As the regulatory form debate has moved into the administrative realm and concrete programs based on alternative techniques have developed, like those in the EPA, the social regulatory agencies have taken center stage. Very basic questions about how the movement for regulatory reform has influenced the manner in which a particular agency carries out its mission, and how the unique characteristics of the organizational structure of an agency and the politics that dominate its inner workings have influenced how, or even whether, it has pursued reform, are therefore quite appropriate objectives for empirical research.

In addition to these two questions that form the heart of the rationale for my research on EPA and emissions trading, this study may uncover information helpful in answering a number of other questions that merit the attention of students of regulation. For example, the question of how the choice of regulatory form is made and why policy makers continue to choose command-and-control approaches now that the efficiency advantages of alternative, market-oriented techniques are widely recognized, puzzles many scholars. Using public choice theory to develop a simple model that concentrates on the preferences of individual firms affected by pollution control regulations, James Buchanan and Gordon Tullock (1975) contend that under existing institutional arrangements, the prevalence of direct regulation in comparison to such alternatives as a penalty tax on pollution can be explained because even those firms directly affected by the regulations prefer them despite their disadvantages. The authors argue that this is so because firms often realize pecuniary gain from direct controls (they may dampen the vitality of competition) and because regulated firms would view a pollution tax as a legislated change in property rights and therefore confiscatory (Buchanan and Tullock 1975: 142–143). On the whole, then, the regulated community will oppose any move away from direct regulation and toward tax schemes.

More recently, a body of research has developed concentrating on legislative choice of regulatory form and why Congress almost invariably chooses to empower administrative agencies to promulgate rules and standards, rather than using market-oriented techniques or existing law and the judicial system (see, for example, Fiorina 1982, 1985, 1986; and McCubbins 1982, 1985). This research explores a number of alternative explanations, including legislator-benefit models, shift-the-responsibility models, legislative rent-seeking models, and legislator uncertainty models, the latter regarded as most promising. As with the research on the reform of social regulation generally, however, the examination of questions about the choice of regulatory form has not given much consideration to the role administrative agencies may play in choosing among alternative regulatory forms, and what factors may influence agency choices in this regard. By examining the legislative background of emissions trading, and by exploring in depth the arguments put forth for and against the program during its development and implementation, the present study may prove helpful in advancing scholarly understanding of both administrative and legislative choice of regulatory form.

Another question of considerable interest to students of regulatory reform focuses on what political issues come to the forefront in major drives to reform regulation. Students of regulation have studied such issues in considerable detail in numerous treatises on regulatory reform, but not very much so with respect to the debate over regulatory form. As I have defined it, regulatory form is about how a regulatory regime should be structured, and what policy instruments should be used to achieve regulatory objectives. One might therefore expect that the most controversial issues in any case of an attempt to alter regulatory forms would center on disagreements over technique. This would appear to be the case with respect to the EPA and emissions trading. Yet the evidence I collected, largely through interviews with many of the decision makers involved in the program, also strongly suggests that beneath the surface, the debate over emissions trading that raged inside the EPA and in the larger environmental policy sphere, including the executive branch, Congress, the states, and the environmental and industrial communities, was about fundamental differences in philosophy and ideology much broader in scope than questions about the intricacies of various administrative techniques.

One additional question, of interest in particular to students of public administration and public policy, for which this study may offer some intriguing answers, concerns the effectiveness of political leadership in public bureaucracies. The American federal bureaucracy, with its curious blend of political and career administrators, has been the subject of considerable inquiry, especially with regard to the questions of how well presidents and their political appointees can control career bureaucrats and thus guide policy toward goals a president seeks. The weight of arguments and evidence seems to fall on the side of relatively circumscribed power to control policy making by career bureaucrats remaining in the hands of political executives.

The results of my research offer a modest counterbalance to the conventional view. Political leadership can have an important impact on policy direction in public bureaucracies. Nevertheless, long-term success in this regard requires advanced planning and comprehension of organizational characteristics to a degree that some of EPA's key political executives could not quite achieve. After laying additional groundwork in chapters 2 and 3, it is the successes and failures of EPA's reformers to which I will turn my attention.

NOTES

1. George Eads and Michael Fix offer observations about the appeal of Reagan's program, similar to the one that follows, at various points in their analysis of the president's "regulatory dilemma." "[D]ifferent people could listen to him promise to do something about social regulation and believe that he was endorsing their favored remedy. Only later, when general statements had to be translated into specific actions, did the inconsistencies become a problem" (Eads and Fix 1984: 95; see also pp. 8, 104–105).

2. On his first full day in office (January 22, 1981), President Reagan created the President's Task Force on Regulatory Relief, chaired by Vice President Bush. The president charged the task force with assembling a list of newly proposed and existing regulations considered wasteful, overly intrusive, and unnecessary, and to seek revisions or withdrawals of such regulations. The task force did in fact produce the planned-for target list of regulations. Critics charged, however, that few of those regulations were changed or eliminated as a result of the task force's work, and many of those that were changed had been targeted for revision anyway. See Wines (1983) and Eads and Fix (1984: chapter 6).

3. I have relied heavily in building my descriptions of the two categories on the following sources: Eads and Fix (1984); Derthick and Quirk (1985); Graymer and Thompson (1982); Meier (1985); and White (1981).

4. This distinction is not especially pure. For example, consumer protection laws are administered by, among other organizations, the Federal Trade Commission and the Consumer Product Safety Commission. Agricultural price supports are administered by the Agricultural Stabilization and Conservation Service in the Department of Agriculture.

5. President Reagan abolished COWPS, RARG, and the Regulatory Council. The Office of Information and Regulatory Affairs (OIRA) in OMB took over the functions of these organizations. Congress created OIRA as part of the Paperwork Reduction Act of 1980 (see Seidman and Gilmour 1986: 131).

6. For key references in the political science literature, see note 1 in chapter 7. Basic references for the economic theory of regulation and its arguments about interest group capture of regulatory agencies include Moore (1961), Stigler (1971), and Posner (1974).

7. Some agencies, OSHA being the most prominent example, have been singled out for very strong criticism because of the way they have carried out their legislative mandates. These agencies have become the targets of major reform efforts. See Kelman (1980, 1981a) for analyses of occupational safety and health regulation and the actions of OSHA. Kelman's research contradicts in some ways my claim that economists have had the study of social regulation and its reform almost exclusively to themselves, but see the discussion that follows in the text. I believe my work fits most readily into the niche carved out by Kelman.

2

THE REGULATORY FORM DEBATE

Presidents and judges, legislators and bureaucrats, businessmen and scholars have worried about and wrangled over regulation in its modern garb for over 100 years. The first order regulatory decision, whether or not to intervene in some economic or social activity, has attracted the lion's share of the energy invested in debate. Yet the second order regulatory decision, what means to employ to carry out the decision to intervene, has hardly been ignored, and attention has intensified over the past two decades. This is especially true in more recent years, when in a number of cases, like environmental regulation, policy makers and the general public have regarded deregulation, reversing the decision to intervene, too drastic a step, and have sought more modest adjustments through regulatory reform.

This chapter offers a primer on the debate that has taken place with respect to regulatory form. The chapter summarizes the various means available to regulators attempting to exert some control over a social or economic activity. The chapter then explores critical areas of disagreement, at both the theoretical and practical levels, concerning what policy instruments are most appropriate for realizing the goals of social regulation. Incentive forms of regulation, derived from microeconomic theory and advocated most persistently by economists, offer policy makers a wide range of optional regulatory devices quite distinct from traditional command and control. Incentive forms of regulation thus have greatly expanded the arena of debate surrounding regulatory form. The story that unfolds in the chapters that follow also highlights economic incentives because the use of incentive schemes was (and remains) a central part of policy changes advocated by regulatory reformers in the EPA. The exploration of the regulatory form debate offered in this chapter therefore serves as a guide to some of the conflicts over regulatory form associated with the development and implementation of emissions trading in the EPA by concentrating on incentive techniques, and considering the advantages and disadvantages of incentives when compared with direct regulation.

ADMINISTERING REGULATION: DIRECTIVE AND INCENTIVE MEANS

Once a legislature or other policy-making body decides to intervene in a specific economic or social activity, it must decide what means ought to be used to achieve the goals it seeks through regulation. Legislators may, for example, choose to use the courts directly to manipulate the behavior of some group of individuals or class of organizations singled out for regulation. Policy makers can put existing laws and the judicial system to use to achieve desired ends, or they can enact new laws that provide the courts the means to impose civil or criminal judgments on recalcitrant parties.

Much more typically, however, legislatures choose to create new administrative organizations or use existing agencies to carry out regulatory mandates, with the courts serving as only secondary instruments of enforcement. Legislators may designate the form of the means the administrative agency is to use to achieve the goals of the regulation in question, or they may leave such decisions up to the agency as it goes about its business of establishing and administering the detailed structure of a regulatory regime. In either case, the responsible decision makers have two basic mechanisms of regulatory control from which to choose. They may choose to control through direct specification or instruction of the regulated party's behavior, or they may attempt to control through rewards that encourage the regulated party to behave as the regulators desire. The critical difference in the essential nature of these control mechanisms is how they shape the environment of choice of regulated parties. Direct specification circumscribes choices of action available to the individuals or groups subject to regulation. Regulation through a strategy of selective rewards or incentives, on the other hand, increases the attractiveness of certain actions that may be chosen from among others by the regulated parties (Mitnick 1982: 140).

Two fundamental forms of regulation are thus at the disposal of regulators: directives and incentives. A simple model of how an administrative agency would organize and operate a regulatory system using either directives or incentives provides a useful way to describe the primary techniques of control available within each form.

In the directives model, public policy objectives are to be achieved by placing direct controls on behavior, that is, directing people to act in specified ways through legislation and administrative commands (hence the familiar label command and control). The process of establishing and operating a command-and-control system typically looks as follows. After the statutory authority is drawn with its specification of the implementing agency, the administrative machinery moves into gear. Usually the administrative agency has substantial discretion in deciding how the mandated objectives are to be achieved, although the enabling legislation may mix such discretion with stipulations regarding specific targets or specific types of technologies to be employed. The agency uses its discretion for a variety of purposes, including clarification of the target group whose behavior is to be altered.

The agency then proceeds to draw up a series of specifications, directions, and prohibitions in the form of rules and standards. The range of choices for action from which the regulated parties can choose when engaging in some social or economic activity is thereby circumscribed. The agency then monitors compliance with its directives. The agency may have either direct power, or indirect power through the courts, to use civil or criminal procedures to halt the activities of those who violate the rules and standards. Thus directives established solely by administrative action nevertheless carry the force of law and individuals and organizations are expected to obey them as they would the law. Finally, the agency may have a variety of other discretionary powers, including exacting fines and hearing appeals for exceptions to its directives.

In sum, rules and standards are the principal tools of control under any system of regulation by directives. The structure of federal air pollution control programs is indicative of regulatory systems relying on rules and standards to alter behavior (see the detailed description of the framework for air pollution control at the federal level provided in chapter 3). Public enterprise, where the activity to be regulated is carried out by a publicly owned and operated entity in some form, is another, more extreme form of direct regulation, which will not be given further attention here. (See Mitnick 1980: 396–401 for an exhaustive treatment of both rules and standards and public enterprise.)

Under the incentives model, the agency seeks to alter the behavior of regulated parties by restructuring rather than overtly limiting the environment of choice. The target population retains the freedom to choose among a wide range of actions, but is encouraged through positive and negative incentives to pick actions that are consonant with the behavior regulators desire. In most instances of regulation by incentives, regulated parties are expected to do what is economically most advantageous, to act, that is, as if they are operating in the marketplace. In short, the agency attempts to use the discipline of the marketplace, under controlled conditions, to steer the choice behavior of regulated parties in one general direction and thus achieve publicly designated ends.

The agency can try to bring this about through one of two general approaches. The first version is to make existing market arrangements operate better by using more effectively key attributes of the market, particularly prices and information. In the second version, market-like arrangements are actually created that mimic "real" markets in the way they generate incentives that encourage certain kinds of behavior. Although an administrative agency is at work in both these versions of the incentives model, the emphasis is on decentralized, self-interest–driven activity guided by the agency through its efforts to structure incentives.

In attempting to use existing markets more effectively, the regulatory authority might provide consumers information on the risks associated with the use of a product, through labeling for example, instead of regulating production or use of the product through direct specifications. This strategy allows consumers themselves to judge the relative costs and benefits of use of a product and thus to adjust their behavior accordingly (Mitnick 1982: 140).

Another regulatory strategy aimed at improving existing market operations encompasses programs to "prime the pump" through subsidies. Subsidies are not always included in catalogues of incentive-based regulatory alternatives. Most economists in fact do not regard subsidies as truly reflecting the central attributes of the incentives model. Subsidies do, however, offer an "economic incentive" in the sense that financial inducements give regulated parties an incentive to take actions desired by the regulatory authority.

In pollution control, subsidies fall into two basic categories: unit subsidies for the reduction of waste discharges, and grants to defray the costs of pollution control equipment (Baumol and Oates 1979: 246–250; Mitnick 1980: 368, 383–385). Equipment grants bear little resemblance to true economic incentives. This form of subsidy limits a polluter's freedom to choose the means for reducing pollution that is most appropriate to a particular production process. Grant-type subsidies also are rarely effective as an incentive unless they represent 100 percent of equipment costs, a very expensive proposition on a large scale. Finally, grants for pollution control equipment do not directly encourage pollution reductions but only something loosely connected to such reductions: the purchase of control equipment.

Unit subsidies for the reduction of discharges, on the other hand, are somewhat more defensible as economic incentives. Firms must take costs into account with unit subsidies because for each unit of pollution a firm fails to reduce, it loses a portion of the subsidy. Economists regard unit subsidies as less effective than true economic incentives because they represent an administrative problem in establishing a benchmark from which unit reductions can be calculated. More importantly, unit subsidies can provide profits to firms that are in reality unprofitable were the costs of pollution internalized to production. Hence, unit subsidies do not in the full sense internalize the social costs of pollution, which is the objective of all economic incentive schemes.

Yet a third form of subsidy flexible enough to be employed either to help defray the costs of pollution control equipment or as a unit subsidy is the tax incentive (see Mitnick 1980: 365–366, 368–371). Tax incentives, or the remission of taxes in a variety of ways, such as through deferrals, deductions, credits, exclusions, or preferred rates, are not normally associated with incentive techniques for pollution control. They may be distinguished from the more familiar effluent or emission tax by the positive (rather than negative) incentive they offer, and by their use of the existing tax system rather than the establishment of a wholly new and independent tax schedule required by an effluent or emission tax. Tax incentives operate in much the same way as subsidies in that regulated firms realize greater financial resources to pursue activities in ways desired by regulators by not having to pay the government a portion of the taxes they would otherwise owe.

A more complex and more direct method of improving market operations, and the most widely advocated approach to using incentives in environmental regulation, is to apply a charge, fee, or tax on effluent or emissions from a polluting firm on a per unit basis. The regulatory authority imposes charges in the amount of the incremental damage one extra unit of pollution causes to the assimilative capacity of the relevant medium (air, water, or land). The unit charges may vary according to the type of pollution, type of industry, and other factors. A charge scheme forces the external social costs of pollution to be internalized into the cost functions of polluters by setting prices on the consumption of the hitherto unpriced assimilative capacity of common property resources (Rothenberg 1974: 209). The tax or fee in effect forces the establishment of a price for pollution administratively, and once the price has been set, the charge system lets the market operate to affect the "supply" of pollution given the established price. With a charge levied on pollution, polluting firms must include it in their operating costs. The firms then have the incentive to reduce pollution to the point at which further reductions are more costly than paying the fee or tax (Kneese and Schultze 1975: 88–90).

An incentive approach structured around principles of achieving mandated air or water quality goals (that is, levels of emissions or effluent) rather than pricing damages involves establishing markets in pollution rights, licenses, or permits. The emissions trading program most closely resembles this second general version of incentive-based regulation (see Tietenberg 1985). Under such an approach for air pollution control, for example, once the total level of emissions compatible with a set of air quality standards is determined, the regulatory authority issues a number of pollution permits or licenses that in total are congruent with the standards (Rothenberg 1974: 210; Baumol and Oates 1979: 250–253). The licenses or permits may be auctioned off, or they may be allocated on the basis of average historical emissions, or by other methods. The market comes into existence as firms buy and sell the permits. The regulatory authority may place some limitations on the trading by setting a limit on how long permits stay in force, or by limiting permit trading, buying, and selling to the same or similar types of pollutants from similar types of firms. Permits covering sulfur dioxide emissions from power plants, for example, may not be traded for particulate emission permits held by steel processors.

Marketable pollution license schemes work by establishing a market mechanism for a commodity that may not have been tradable previously, thereby providing an incentive to firms to reduce their emissions. In other words, firms that can reduce their emissions relatively cheaply will have the incentive to do so because they can hold on to the excess licenses to provide for future expansion, or they can sell the excess permits to other firms that face much higher abatement costs.

Finally, defining or clarifying who has the right to engage in certain activities such as generating pollution, and in what quantities, can rectify some of the shortcomings associated with direct regulation (Rothenberg 1974: 199–200; Baumol and Oates 1979: 221–223). By "privatizing" rights and allowing transactions involving them to take place in market settings, some of the benefits of other incentive approaches such as reducing information demands and transaction costs (see the next section) can be realized. The problem with such an approach is again that social costs are not completely internalized. The rights entail third-party effects or spillovers themselves, imposing costs that are not borne by the producer. Hence, two-party transactions involving the rights affect numerous other parties, "because the 'rights' refer not to pollution effects but to intervening processes . . . whose damage effects vary with the number and identity of the polluters as well as the victims" (Rothenberg 1974: 200). Schemes for defining and clarifying property rights and schemes for setting up markets in pollution permits or licenses differ in important ways, yet they are closely intertwined, and as will become amply clear later (see chapter 6), questions about property rights inevitably follow attempts to use pollution control schemes structured on the principle of markets in pollution licenses or permits.

CRITICAL ISSUES IN THE REGULATORY FORM DEBATE

Most of the advantages economists claim for incentive approaches to regulation grow out of the comparison of the incentives model, with its focus on an agency structuring the environment of choice of regulated parties, and the directives model, with its emphasis on forcing regulated parties to make prescribed choices. Such analyses frequently contrast the operation of command-and-control systems in practice with the theory of incentive-based regulation, there being few incentive systems in operation that would permit a reasonable comparison of the two basic forms of regulation on a practical basis. The best way to get a flavor for the debate over regulatory form is to examine the relative advantages and disadvantages of incentive schemes. What follows then is a survey of the critical issues in the regulatory form debate concentrating on incentive approaches. This review is by no means exhaustive, but it does cover the arguments that seem most attractive to the combatants, specifically with respect to pollution control.[1] I begin with a discussion of incentive advantages, then consider the disadvantages of regulation by incentives, highlighting the relative value of directives along the way.

The Advantages of Incentives

As one might expect, given the microeconomic origins of the incentives model, many of the superior qualities associated with regulation by incentives concern the greater economy this approach to regulation has to offer in a number of areas. Nevertheless, advocates of incentive-based regulation have claimed other advantages, ranging from administrative simplicity to normative preeminence.

Efficiency. The same policy objectives—cleaner air, safer workplaces, less traffic congestion—can be achieved at lower cost through incentives than through directives. In the case of air pollution, for example, production processes and the costs of production vary widely across firms and industries. Hence the costs of reducing the emissions for a particular pollutant by a designated amount will also vary. It is more efficient for firms that find reducing the emissions of a particular pollutant less costly to undertake greater degrees of control. Incentive systems encourage such behavior because firms that find pollution control relatively cheap face important financial incentives (the avoidance of a fee or the opportunity to generate excess pollution permits that can be sold to the highest bidder). In contrast, directive systems tied to uniform standards and rules require all firms to reduce the emissions of a designated pollutant to commensurate levels, regardless of cost. The resources invested in pollution control are thus allocated inefficiently. More generally, incentives are more efficient because market forces encourage firms to seek the most cost-effective ways of doing business.

Flexibility. Incentives decentralize regulatory decisions so that, as in the case of pollution control, each firm can choose the mix of controls, and charges to be paid or licenses to be purchased, that is optimum for its circumstances. The flexibility associated with decentralized decision making under an incentive system also makes incentives more conducive to change, should adjustments in a pollution control program be necessary. In particular, incentives are easier to change because they do not achieve the norm- or law-like status of directives. Furthermore, incentives can accommodate more gradual change because they can be fine tuned to a greater degree than directives. The possibilities for fine tuning and thus gradual change also make regulatory adjustments under an incentive system less costly.

Effectiveness. By harnessing the economic self-interest of regulated parties, and thus the discipline of the marketplace, incentives are more likely than directives to be effective in reaching such regulatory goals as cleaner air or water. Firms cannot avoid the imposition of emission or effluent charges, or the need to purchase pollution permits in a permit market, unless they reduce their pollution discharges. No amount of special pleading can exempt firms from the impact of market forces (unless, of course, regulators cave in and grant special protections to individual firms or whole industries). Thus basic considerations of economic survival drive polluting firms in the direction of regulatory compliance. The strong medicine administered by market discipline may make a regulatory regime based on incentives successful, even when necessary enforcement mechanisms are flawed or nonexistent.

Technological Innovation. Directives, especially so-called input or design standards, discourage technological innovation. Once regulated parties have met the designated standards, they face no incentives to seek new, more efficient techniques to achieve the same results. The incentive under command and control is simply to conform. In contrast, incentives offer benefits for innovation. The regulatory authority structures the decision environment so that taxes, fees, or charges decline, tax benefits increase, or more licenses or permits become available to sell. Firms thus seek such financial rewards by exploring a variety of administrative and technological solutions for reducing their pollution control costs. The incentive to innovate remains in force until the marginal cost of technological changes and other innovations exceeds the marginal cost of forgoing benefits offered by the incentives.

Information Use. One of the principal attributes of the market is its efficiency in processing and distributing information. Prices provide accurate and timely signals to market participants about the costs of resources, thus insuring that efficient allocation decisions are made. Further, only the information that is needed for each individual decision is collected and used, thus economizing on a costly resource. A major criticism of command and control is that it cannot match the information processing advantages of the market. Under a system of directives, the administrative agency must attempt to collect all the information that all parties subject to regulation would need to make decisions about resource allocation so that it can set standards accordingly. Under various forms of incentive regulation, however, the market performs its normal function of information processor. Resources are therefore not wasted either in centrally collecting all the information or in misallocating resources because of poor or incomplete information.

Transaction Costs. Regulation by directives, with discretionary bureaucracies hedged in by legal constraints and actively creating complex systems of commands and prohibitions, stimulates considerable bargaining, mediation, compromise, and litigation between the regulatory authority and regulated parties. Such methods for transacting business can be extremely costly. A system of incentives achieves the same results through a combination of simple transactions between an administrative agency and a regulated firm (for example, paying a tax) and between private parties (for example, buying and selling pollution permits). Neither transaction requires elaborate efforts by the agency nor will the private firms insist on employing armies of high-priced attorneys skilled in high-stakes special pleading.

Administrative Complexity. Command and control requires a large, often legally and organizationally complex administrative apparatus to write, coordinate, and enforce rules and standards. A system of incentives, on the other hand, is virtually self-enforcing. Because a system of incentives attempts to harness economic self-interest in existing markets or those created by regulators, externally imposed decisions pushing regulated parties toward a designated objective are not needed. Likewise, externally imposed penalties to force compliance with rules and standards are unnecessary. Economic gain or loss is the principal decision directive and enforcement device and it is internal to the system. A smaller administrative organization therefore is needed because the demands for information collection, detailed specification of permissible behavior, and enforcement are reduced. The principal task of this smaller organization is occasionally to monitor progress toward policy objectives. Society thus also realizes efficiency gains as fewer administrative resources are consumed by regulation.

Intrusiveness. If one argues that minimizing government involvement in private affairs is desirable, then incentives are preferable. Regulation by incentives does not eliminate government intrusion, but it does attempt to minimize intrusion by using existing institutions in which decentralized, self-directed decision making is dominant. Incentive systems encourage private decision making toward public ends relatively free of government paternalism.

Egalitarianism. Politically volatile questions about just distributions of wealth and valuable resources often accompany many of the ends society seeks through social regulation. The political strife that occurs over such questions often derails society's efforts to make critical collective decisions. Markets are relatively passionless, however. As social choice mechanisms they allow societies to sidestep dangerous political questions. Markets impose a very harsh but effective form of egalitarianism, survival of the most efficient. All parties are subject to this single standard of performance. Those found wanting will fall by the wayside as society moves toward achieving crucial objectives.

The Disadvantages of Incentives

Central to the attempts of regulatory reformers to devise incentive systems is the argument that the market is a remarkably effective and adaptive institution for making complex collective decisions. Reformers argue that with the increasing complexity of the problems reaching the public agenda, and the considerable social cost associated with regulation by directives, government would be wise to adapt features of the market as part of its arsenal of devices for achieving public policy objectives. This argument has come under intense scrutiny and critics have identified a number of weaknesses in the case for regulation by incentives. Many of the criticisms aimed at incentive-based regulation are based upon questions of practice or technique. Some criticisms are, however, rooted in questions of politics and morality.

Practicability. That incentive systems will actually work in practice is not a forgone conclusion, especially because we have so little practical experience with regulation by incentives. The practicability critique has a number of facets. The principal problem in setting up an emission tax scheme, for example, is the level at which the tax should be set for different pollutants and different industries. Setting the tax level requires some knowledge of the link between particular actions taken by the regulated firms and the desired results—improved air quality. The regulatory authority may need to calculate damage functions for the various pollutants, but damage functions are particularly hard to define. Regulators may also need detailed information about production cost functions for various industries if it is deemed important to know the impact of the tax on designated industries. Yet such information requirements run counter to the information processing advantages claimed for incentives. Avoiding the burdensome information demands implied in the estimations of damage functions and production costs by setting a uniform tax may lead to gross inefficiencies, economic disruption, and, worst of all, undercontrol, resulting in environmental damage and threats to public health.

Another facet of the practicability critique concerns monitoring procedures. Effluent fees require some method for assessing and collecting the fees. Marketable permits require some method by which regulators can determine the number of permits to which a firm is entitled. Continuous discharge monitors may be installed to calculate the tax a firm owes, but the technological requirements for continuous discharge monitoring exceed the capacities of most current systems. Self-reporting may be used, but honesty and reliability have traditionally been the weak links in such arrangements. Yet a third tool, especially important for the success of marketable permit systems, is the use of dispersion modeling. However, full dispersion modeling is quite expensive, data for such modeling is often flawed or nonexistent, and the accuracy of such modeling exercises often has been challenged.

Certainty and Effectiveness. Decentralized and relatively uncontrollable markets make for highly uncertain policy tools. Some of the principal attractions of incentive systems also make it especially uncertain that regulators will be able to steer regulated firms toward the appropriate policy objectives, particularly under emergency conditions. Furthermore, clearly stated policy goals must exist for incentives to work, a state of affairs rarely achieved. In contrast, command and control, with the coercive powers of the state behind it, is likely to have more direct, more certain, more rapid effects and be more effective in an emergency. Numerically measurable standards give polluters and regulators unambiguous and clearly enforceable rules concerning what each polluter must do. Standards also help to make environmental quality goals explicit and provide a means of measuring progress toward achieving the goals. Directives thus create a predictable, stable, clearly defined regulatory environment, a feature businesses subject to regulation find particularly attractive. Finally, directives may be more effective because there is no limit to their specificity, and directives are less likely to lose effectiveness with repeated application.

Technological Innovation. The promise of significant technological innovation under regulation by incentives may depend on some dubious assertions about the causes and sources of innovation. Some evidence indicates that input costs, which usually include the costs of compliance with regulations, only modestly influence decisions regarding research and development, that is, innovation. The structure of an industry appears to matter much more. Moreover, the major source of innovation is more likely to be suppliers rather than end users—the regulated firms. Firms in the business of designing, manufacturing, and supplying pollution control equipment are more likely to generate innovative control techniques than those firms using control technology. Supply firms are also not likely to be affected by switches in regulatory strategies.

Administrative Costs and Complexity. The automatic enforcement features of regulation by incentives may reduce the need for elaborate administration and enforcement organizations. Nevertheless, the structure of an effluent charge system or a market in pollution licenses may require the introduction of a second set of administrative and enforcement bureaucracies, or regulators may be forced to perform a second specialized function for which they have not been trained. In an effluent charge system, for example, not only would some semblance of the existing regulatory bureaucracy still be required for monitoring purposes, but a revenue-collecting bureaucracy, such as the Internal Revenue Service, would also be needed. The double-reporting requirements and jurisdictional confusion of such a system could create a red tape nightmare that would make the current system of regulation by directives seem simple in comparison. Likewise, a market in pollution licenses might require a bureaucracy like the Securities and Exchange Commission to handle the securities aspects of the licenses, as well as tracking and verifying the sale of licenses, and the negotiations over such sales. If not undertaken by a separate bureacracy, regulators would find a major new task such as this added to their existing workload.

Egalitarianism. Under regulation by incentives, equity is essentially synonymous with efficiency. Such an equity norm has powerful arguments in its favor. It is not at all clear, however, that efficiency is a universal, or even widely accepted, norm for public policy. In contrast to incentives, regulation by directives emphasizes fairness and equity by treating large classes of such target groups as polluters equally. Such is the equity concept that underlies the application of a uniform pollution control standard. Equal treatment as a policy norm may be more widely accepted than efficiency. An unequal distribution of burdens and benefits may be acceptable to individuals and groups subject to regulation in the name of equal treatment, while regulated parties may not be willing to support an unequal distribution of costs and benefits from regulation in the name of efficiency.

Morality. Regulation by incentives is more likely to become hopelessly entangled in moral issues. Using the market as a public policy device raises questions about who ought to own objects valued by society, about how values ought to be assigned to social objects, and about what sorts of motives and actions should be encouraged. Such issues may serve to hamper the full and effective operation of an incentive system or they may block implementation of the system altogether. Moreover, the political costs of overcoming moral opposition to a system of regulation by incentives may prove prohibitive.

Legitimacy and National Commitment. Regulation by directives more clearly demonstrates a national commitment to policy goals with broad public support, like those of protecting public health and the environment, by dedicating the legitimate authority and resources of the federal government to such efforts. In addition, the rules formulated as a central part of direct regulation tend to achieve the status of norms, thus according them considerable collective support and legitimacy. The need for coercive enforcement measures therefore may be reduced. This may lessen enforcement and other administrative costs, and compliance may still be attained even when an enforcement apparatus is faulty. Neither the acceptance of incentives at a systemic level or their recognition as norms has occurred, nor is this likely to happen because of practical, political, or moral objections. Hence elaborate enforcement mechanisms with the means to calculate and impose penalties, and the accompanying costs of such administrative devices, will still be required for any system of regulation by incentives.

CONCLUSION

Questions about what form of regulation to employ in pursuit of important health, safety, and environmental policy objectives have ranged far beyond the relative abstractness and obscurity of debate in academic forums. The regulatory form debate has become an important item on the agendas of both legislatures and executive agencies. Decision makers thus have been forced to grapple with the claims and counterclaims of advocates of both the principal approaches to social regulation. How the regulatory form debate has been played out with respect to air pollution control in Congress, but more importantly in the EPA, now becomes the central focus of this study.

NOTE

1. The literature on regulatory form, particularly concerning the use of economic incentives, is quite substantial. I relied on the following sources to organize the discussion in the text: Anderson et al. (1977); Baumol and Oates (1979); Dales (1968); Eads and Fix (1984: 101–104); Kelman (1981); Kneese and Schultze (1975); Majone (1975 and 1976); Marcus, Sommers, and Morris (1982); Meier (1985: 288–289); Mitnick (1980: chapters 6–8); Rose-Ackerman (1973, 1977); Schelling (1983); Schultze (1977); Tietenberg (1985); Wenner (1978); and White (1981: chapter 3).

3

CONGRESS AND ECONOMIC INCENTIVES

Although this study is principally concerned with efforts to transform regulatory programs in an administrative agency, it is always important to keep in mind the broader environment within which significant policy reform by administrative agents takes place. Of special consequence are the characteristics of enabling statutes, and the antecedents of administrative action identifiable in legislative discussion and debate. This is especially critical in the present case, because far from ignoring the possible use of incentive schemes, Congress gave the issue considerable attention, yet failed to provide anything more than minimal, largely rhetorical endorsement of economic incentives when it enacted a series of refinements to the regulatory structure for air pollution control in 1977.

The actions Congress took in both 1970 and 1977 forced regulatory reformers in the EPA to squeeze out of a tightly drawn command-and-control framework for pollution control the statutory authority necessary to accomplish an agenda of incentive-based reform. As subsequent chapters will show, the efforts of EPA political and career executives to introduce economic incentive ideas into the agency's air pollution control programs were at least partially successful because of the reformers' strategy of concentrating on change in the internal political dynamics and organizational character of the agency as the essential vehicle for reform. Ironically, these same factors, internal politics and organizational character, proved to be the major obstacles to ultimate success for the regulatory reform movement in the EPA.

The objective of this chapter, then, is to describe the legislative context surrounding EPA's emissions trading program and the internal organizational politics associated with its development. The chapter provides an overview of the complex structure of air pollution control regulation established by law and administrative action. The overview is in no way exhaustive, however. Instead, it concentrates on stationary-source air pol-

lution control, and in particular on those parts of the regulatory framework
that are the targets of the reform effort embodied in emissions trading.

The chapter also provides a rough chronology of congressional discussion, debate, and action on various proposals to incorporate incentive-based
approaches to air pollution control into an evolving regulatory framework.
As the reader will discover, evidence from committee hearings and floor
debates strongly suggests that some arguments about why Congress has
been extremely reluctant to endorse in legislation incentive-based approaches to air pollution regulation are open to question, and other arguments may only partially explain the lack of success thus far experienced
by legislative proposals for using incentives in pollution control.

THE REGULATORY STRUCTURE FOR AIR POLLUTION CONTROL

The Clean Air Act is the basic law governing America's national effort
to improve and protect air quality. Congress first passed a Clean Air Act
in 1963, but amended the statute so substantially in both 1970 and 1977 that
the complex, detailed, commandful character of the present framework
scarcely resembles the meager provisions contained in the original law.

The foundation of the present structure is an action-forcing strategy directed toward achieving, by specified dates, National Ambient Air Quality
Standards (NAAQS). These standards specify maximum allowable concentrations of common pollutants in the air, with any pollution levels above
the standards considered threats to public health and welfare. The Clean
Air Act requires EPA to set these standards, and requires states to develop
pollution abatement programs to achieve them. EPA reviews, approves,
and financially assists state programs, but if a state fails to act or develops
an inadequate program, EPA can develop its own program for the state.
Federal financial aid for highways and sewage treatment plants can be withheld from noncomplying states, and permits for construction of major new
pollution sources can be blocked. In addition to providing for clean-up of
"dirty air" regions, the Clean Air Act protects from significant future deterioration areas in which air is cleaner than national standards, particularly
national parks and wilderness areas (Liroff 1986: 19–20).

The statutory and programmatic detail behind this summary description
of the Clean Air Act reveals the dramatic changes and redirections in the
philosophical underpinnings supporting air pollution control that began
with the passage of the 1970 amendments and continued in earnest with
the adoption of additional amendments in 1977. These philosophical shifts
should be understood properly, at least in part, as arising from Congress's
recognition that past applications of command and control were inadequate
and disappointing. In particular, Congress identified a number of glaring
deficiencies and tried to overcome them by introducing innovations in 1970

and refinements in 1977. The most significant deficiencies were: (1) a lack of clearly defined objectives; (2) difficulties in relating individual emitters to effects; (3) poor mechanisms for stimulating technological development; and (4) the tendency toward perpetual delay (U.S. Senate 1975: 1514–1515).

To provide unambiguous objectives, for example, Congress sought to define clearly acceptable air quality by establishing air quality standards for "criteria" pollutants, those pollutants, in other words, for which EPA would document the research and health criteria used in setting the standards.[1] Congress empowered EPA to set the level of concentration allowable in the atmosphere for each pollutant and required the agency to incorporate an adequate margin of safety. Costs were not to be taken into consideration.

Congress intended the *primary* standards for the criteria pollutants, the working objectives in the law, to protect public health directly and thus regarded them as the realistic targets of air pollution control efforts. The lawmakers intended the *secondary* standards to protect public welfare, including economic and aesthetic considerations, such as visibility and damage to property and livestock, from known or anticipated effects. These standards are the law's ultimate goals.

EPA set both primary and secondary standards for the NAAQS at levels intended to protect the most vulnerable groups in society, including the elderly, children, and asthmatics, by relying on a "threshold myth" (Freeman 1978: 31–33). The threshold concept holds that exposure to a criteria pollutant for a specified length of time but below a specified level does not pose a significant threat to human health. Considerable medical research and regulatory experience has called into question the threshold concept for a number of the criteria pollutants (Lave and Omenn 1981: 14–15). Nevertheless, the structure based on the threshold concept remains largely intact.

Congress attempted to address difficulties in tracing the effects of pollution back to individual emitting sources by placing the responsibility with the states and by creating an elaborate planning mechanism in the 1970 amendments. A state is required to create and submit for EPA approval a State Implementation Plan (SIP) for meeting and maintaining the NAAQS in its share of the 247 Air Quality Control Regions (AQCRs) lying within its boundaries. Typically, a state's SIP contains a variety of means to maintain the link between polluters and the impact of their pollutants, including: inventories of emission sources and monitoring of air quality for the purpose of planning pollution control strategies; programs to issue permits for existing sources, specifying permissible levels of emissions and, if reductions are necessary, dates by which reductions are to be achieved; monitoring of source compliance via inspections, reviews of records, or sampling of emissions and fuels; enforcement action against noncomplying sources; and review and permitting of proposed new sources of pollution (Liroff 1986: 18).

The conceptual ideal underlying SIPs is that a state could devise an ideally cost-effective abatement plan for each of its AQCRs by using its nearly complete information about all emission sources, about the relationship between emissions from these sources and ambient air quality in an AQCR, and about the costs of control and technologies available for reducing emissions. The state could then process this information and devise an economically efficient program for achieving the ambient standards in each AQCR (Liroff 1986: 20).

Under the SIP provision (section 110 of the Clean Air Act), EPA established procedures for the content, deadlines, submission, and revision of SIPs.- However, states retained considerable initiative and discretion in creating and carrying out the SIPs. The 1970 legislation set a deadline of May 1975 to achieve the ambient standards. Yet the states had only nine months to prepare their SIPs following EPA's initial publication of the standards, and most states had only small, inexpert pollution control agency staffs. With most state agencies overwhelmed by the technically complex requirements and the short time frame, the outcome was inevitable: many states missed-the statutory deadline.

Congress responded by tightening the SIP provisions in 1977, requiring states to implement all reasonably available control measures as expeditiously as possible, and insisting that states show reasonable further progress in emission reductions, especially for existing sources in regions where one or more of the ambient standards were consistently violated (so-called "nonattainment areas"). Specifically, the legislation and subsequent EPA regulations required SIPs to address: (1) the protection of ambient air quality in PSD areas (Prevention of Significant Deterioration areas, where the NAAQS have been attained) through control of new and existing sources; and (2) achievement of the NAAQS in nonattainment areas also by control of new and existing pollution sources.

In tackling the problem of poor mechanisms for stimulating new technological development, which would provide the control techniques states could use in SIPs, Congress created the most complex and controversial elements in the Clean Air Act. The 1970 amendments created New Source Performance Standards (NSPS) for the control of emissions from new or substantially expanded or modified stationary sources. NSPS specified emission standards rather than air quality results and were based on the philosophy of best available technology.

Despite what the name implies, however, NSPS are not true performance standards, in which the regulatory body establishes an objective and the means to attain it are left to the regulated parties. NSPS are instead pure emission standards or input standards, that is, the regulatory body defines an objective in detail and directs the regulated party to use only those means so defined to achieve the designated objective. NSPS emphasize control by technological input, and are what has come to be called "technology forcing" because Congress considers them achievable, but not necessarily routinely achievable at the time of adoption with currently available technology.

Hence, NSPS force polluters to develop new technology to achieve ambient standards.

Under NSPS, EPA can take costs into consideration when specifying the technological control requirements. EPA did just that when it proceeded to implement NSPS on an industry-by-industry basis. This approach to implementing NSPS is historically important because the germ of the impetus for the development of emissions trading can be found in the battles over the NSPS for the smelting industry EPA issued in 1972 (see chapter 4).

In contrast to the tight control over new and modified sources maintained by the federal government, Congress gave the states much greater discretion in controlling emissions from existing sources. EPA required states to submit SIPs specifying the emission limits for existing sources in each AQCR. The statute and regulations tied requirements for control of existing sources directly to the NAAQS. Existing-source standards are thus air quality standards or output (true performance) standards emphasizing control by limit or ceiling because the regulatory body explicitly defines the end or output, but regulated parties can choose the means to achieve the designated end.

In 1977, following renewed concern about threats to pristine air areas and anxiety over the lack of progress in attaining the NAAQS, new legislation and regulations tightened a number of standards. For PSD areas, EPA set ceilings on allowable increments of particulate matter and sulfur dioxide. Also, Congress required adoption of Best Available Control Technology (BACT) for new or substantially modified sources. BACT is at least as stringent as NSPS. For the control of new or modified sources in nonattainment areas, Congress required emission offsets, discussed in more detail later in this chapter and in chapter 4. More importantly, Congress also imposed Lowest Achievable Emissions Rate (LAER) standards for new sources in nonattainment areas. LAER is the most stringent standard. It requires technology superior to the advanced technology normally required by NSPS, and costs are given less weight in LAER than in NSPS. Congress also required existing sources in nonattainment areas to apply a less stringent technological standard than NSPS called RACT, or Reasonably Available Control Technology.

Finally, in coming to grips with the problem of perpetual delay in compliance, Congress settled upon two methods: deadlines and penalties. The original deadlines in the 1970 amendments were surprisingly stringent. States were to achieve primary NAAQS by May 31, 1975. Congress allowed for some extensions to mid–1977. Because very few areas of the country had met the air quality standards by the time the Clean Air Act was reauthorized in 1977, Congress reset the deadlines to December 31, 1982, with some extensions to December 31, 1987.

To give the enforcement effort more teeth, Congress provided penalties for noncompliance. The 1970 amendments provided only for criminal penalties, which limited their effectiveness because EPA administrators considered the onus of criminality too severe. The 1977 amendments therefore provided the EPA administrator with authority to issue administrative compliance orders and delayed compliance orders backed up by civil "noncompliance" penalties of up to $25,000 per day or up to the net economic benefit realized by a firm as a result of its failure to comply with the law.

Taken together, the 1970 and 1977 Clean Air Act amendments clearly establish and reinforce a demanding mechanism for cleaning up and protecting the nation's air that readily draws on a command-and-control model of the regulatory process. EPA tells states and polluters in considerable detail how pollution should be abated down to the smallest emission sources in complex facilities. Where EPA leaves discretion to the states, the states often dictate to polluters how reductions in emissions should be achieved.

The regulatory structure established by the Clean Air Act, in amendments enacted by Congress and regulations issued by the Environmental Protection Agency, has come under frequent attack. Critics have objected to specific program elements as well as to the general command-and-control concept that lies at the heart of program design (see chapter 2 for an enumeration of such criticisms). In response to mounting dissatisfaction, scholars, legislators, and administrators have proposed an array of alternatives, the foremost being economic incentive schemes, to amend or replace the established framework. The next section examines the record of legislative consideration of such proposals.

CONGRESSIONAL CONSIDERATION OF ECONOMIC INCENTIVES

The manner in which Congress has considered and acted upon incentive-based regulatory reform proposals is a telling prelude to the progress, and impact, such proposals have made within the EPA. Moreover, the public record on congressional action in this area of social regulation provides considerable insight into the ways legislators frame the issues surrounding a policy question with far reaching consequences.

Before the federal government got involved, local and state governments attempted to control air pollution mainly through enforcement of nuisance laws (Jones 1975: 21–29). Early federal air pollution control policy provided for a very restricted federal role. Legislation passed in 1955, 1960, and 1967 limited federal government activity largely to research and development (Jones 1975: 69–84; Bonine 1975). In the event of an acute air pollution control problem, the federal government could call a regional conference, including federal, state, and local officials and industry representatives. Together they would try to find a solution to the crisis. On the whole, then, the relationship between industry and the federal government was at most self-regulatory, perhaps even *laissez-faire*, but certainly not adversarial, a far cry from what was to come in 1970.

About the time that the federal government first entered the air pollution control policy arena, the idea of a tax on pollution emissions had become widely accepted, at least among economists. Because the federal regulatory structure was so slight, however, and because environmental quality had not yet become a *cause célèbre*, economists had little reason to press their policy ideas on an inattentive Congress. Consequently, no indication of any legislative consideration of economic incentive approaches to air pollution control appears in the public record before 1970.

The first substantial opportunity for congressional consideration of proposals to use incentive-based regulatory devices arose with the drafting of the 1970 amendments to the Clean Air Act. Again, the opportunity emerged in part as the result of acute dissatisfaction in Congress over the deficiencies of the regulatory approach applied up to that time. The dissatisfaction involved in particular the pace of progress in bringing air pollution under control (Bonine 1975: 8). In addition, Jones (1975: 175–176) argues that, given the traditionally strong state-local involvement in the air pollution regulatory structure, one should have expected an incremental clarification and expansion of federal authority. Yet a much more dramatic change occurred. Federal regulatory activism and the seeds that were sown for an adversarial relationship between government and industry resulted, in Jones's view, from a change in decision-maker perceptions of public concern about air pollution. Jones also cites the remarkable expansion of involvement by organized, activist citizen groups, especially those led by Ralph Nader (also see Marcus 1980b: chapter 2), supporting strong air pollution control policy. With this very forceful public pressure, "no mere increment of authority was acceptable" (Jones 1975: 175).

The "speculative augmentation" of policy Jones identifies could have provided the perfect environment for introducing a wide array of significant, even radical, proposals for changing the modest command-and-control system in place at the time. The dramatic shift in decision-maker perceptions regarding the importance of air pollution, and what should be done about it, was not accompanied by greater attention to the possibilities of alternative regulatory strategies using economic incentives, however. Congress debated cost considerations at great length, especially with respect to the new source performance standards. Lawmakers also discussed providing states the freedom to explore alternative control strategies and incorporated this idea into the state implementation plan provision.[2] Yet the hearings and debates preceding passage of the 1970 legislation contain no explicit discussion of charges, taxes, or any other incentive scheme.

The most significant rumblings regarding the economic approach to pollution control at this time emanated from the executive branch. For example, as early as 1966, the chairman of the president's Council of Economic

Advisors had organized staff committees to consider various proposals for using economic incentives for industrial pollution abatement, especially effluent charges (Cannon 1977). Also, in his 1970 State of the Union address, President Nixon proposed a lengthy list of air pollution programmatic changes that included "pricing goods to include the costs of producing and disposing of them without damage to the environment" (Jones 1975: 180).

Not until after the passage of the Clean Air Amendments of 1970 did more substantial legislative activity regarding incentive schemes, mostly effluent charges, ensue. Legislators may have considered the strengthened federal role in pollution control they developed to have been so extreme in and of itself as to rule out consideration of even more "radical" proposals like those incorporating incentive-based techniques. Whatever the reasons behind Congress's failure to consider a role for economic incentives in its blanket restructuring of air pollution regulation, the dramatic policy change wrought in 1970, especially the broadened scope, intrusiveness, and cost of the new regulatory apparatus, forced policy analysts and policy makers alike to give much greater attention to the potential political and economic impact of an activist federal role in environmental policy. A consideration of economic incentives became very much a part of this increased attention. During the first five years under the new structure, discussion and debate about incentive schemes, mostly charges and taxes, took place in a number of legislative forums.

Early Deliberation on Incentive Ideas: 1970–1975

In 1971, the Joint Economic Committee (JEC) of Congress held a wide-ranging series of hearings on the efficiency of government, including a consideration of economic incentives for pollution control (U.S. JEC 1971). A number of well-known economists, Charles Schultze and Allen Kneese among them, testified before the committee, concentrating almost exclusively on water pollution control. Given the focus of the committee's probe—efficiency—and the background of most of the witnesses, the fundamental message of the testimony was clear: a nearly wholesale endorsement of economic incentives as a "better" way to regulate pollution.

The hearings record is not clear on the extent to which members of the Joint Economic Committee found the ideas of the expert witnesses appealing. Even if the committee did decide to pursue the ideas in legislation, however, the JEC's power to legislate was limited. Other committees, and both houses of Congress, duly empowered to authorize legislation, would have to act on such ideas.

Such action did follow, as an expanded and much more revealing exchange of views about the use of economic incentives for water pollution control took place during Senate floor debate on the Federal Water Pollution Control Act Amendments of 1972. Senator William Proxmire (D-WI) proposed an amendment to incorporate an effluent charge system into the regulatory structure established by the 1972 legislation. Proxmire defended effluent charges on the following grounds: (1) charges were easier to enforce; (2) a charge system required less bureaucracy; (3) the system gave more flexibility to industry; and (4) better clean-up would be achieved faster because the system used the stimulus of the marketplace incentive.

Senator Edmund Muskie (D-ME), the Senate's "Mr. Environment" and the principal craftsman of most of the major environmental initiatives in the Senate, attacked Proxmire's amendment. Muskie disparaged effluent charges on the following grounds: (1) such systems had no proven record of actual use. Examples from the Ruhr River valley in Germany were not acceptable because the system in place there was not a true effluent fee system. It was, instead, a user fee system used to finance creation of a water distribution system; (2) an effluent charge system promised that *more*, not *fewer*, bureaucratic agents, in addition to the ones already in place, would be introduced into the pollution control regulatory structure. These bureaucrats, perhaps from the Internal Revenue Service, would be concerned with the revenue generated by the scheme. Muskie wondered how decisions about generating revenue would affect decisions about the proper level of pollution control; and (3) Muskie objected to the Proxmire amendment by stating that he did not think it wise to give industry the option of polluting for a fee. Eventually a number of other senators joined the debate. Senator Howard Baker (R-TN) made the most penetrating observation. "That is the point that bothers me about the Senator's amendment . . . that the Senator from Wisconsin is suggesting that the only laws the people of the United States take seriously are the internal revenue laws, and that is not so" (U.S. CRS 1977: 675). The Proxmire amendment failed.

In the case of air pollution control, legislative activity on economic incentives began much more slowly. In 1622 pages of testimony from the 1972 Senate oversight hearings on the Clean Air Act, White (1976) found that committee members asked only two questions about incentive schemes, focusing again on charges. The extent of the remarks on this subject totalled three pages, and those being questioned rejected the concept of an emissions charge or pollution tax.

Similarly, during the years 1971–1973, the Nixon administration made a series of legislative proposals, only slightly altered from one year to the next, which included taxes or fees in three air pollution control initiatives: parking surcharges, gasoline lead additives, and sulfur oxide emissions. The proposals never got out of the House Ways and Means Committee. The opposition in the committee, especially from Chairman Wilbur Mills (D-AR), was to the concept of using a revenue-raising device to control pollution. Mills objected to any use of the tax code other than raising revenue (Lane 1977: 685; Irwin and Liroff 1974: 58–79; Gamse 1982: 159–161).

During 1973 testimony, a Senate panel questioned EPA administrator

William Ruckleshaus regarding his needs for greater enforcement flexibility and the use of alternative enforcement strategies. Ruckleshaus proceeded to mention effluent and emission charges and other economic "incentives and disincentives." Ruckleshaus ruled out the possibility of their use, citing many problems associated with them, including getting Congress to accept them (White 1976).

Finally, in 1975, during early Senate hearings on reauthorization of the Clean Air Act, economist Larry Ruff presented testimony on various tax and charge schemes (U.S. Senate 1975). Ruff's discussion with the senators began by focusing on the relative merits of a true tax scheme versus an "excess emission penalty" modeled on the so-called Connecticut Plan (see chapter 4). Ruff's list of advantages for incentives repeated the familiar litany of advantages of incentive approaches to pollution control advanced chiefly by economists over the past 20 years (see chapter 2). The senators, however, did not even bother to debate the relative merits of economic incentives and direct regulation, as the discussion quickly shifted to concerns about specific control technologies and about the problems of states with large deposits of high-sulfur coal.

Three facts stand out starkly in the evidence presented so far regarding attention to economic incentives in legislative deliberations. First, it is clear that many members of Congress had been exposed to the ideas behind the use of economic incentives in pollution control, through various legislative forums, between 1970 and 1975. Senators and representatives heard testimony on the merits, and occasionally on objections to, economic incentives. Lawmakers also engaged in dialogue with expert witnesses and colleagues regarding the use of incentive schemes.

Second, the Senate was in the vanguard of shaping pollution control policy at this time. In large part, but not exclusively, because of Edmund Muskie's own stance regarding effluent charges and other incentives, the Senate and the Congress as a whole repeatedly rejected that approach. Moreover, interest in discussing the merits of economic incentives was clearly beginning to wane in the Senate by 1975.

Finally, the charge concept dominated all discussions, at least in legislative forums, about the use of economic incentives in pollution control. The most likely explanation is that pollution charges dominated the preferences of economists as well. Hence, when economists were invited to testify before various congressional committees, they invariably advocated the adoption of some version of a charge scheme.

The Reauthorization Debates: 1975–1977

Congressional exposure and attention to economic incentive ideas expanded, but other circumstances changed fundamentally, as the pace of activity surrounding reauthorization of the Clean Air Act quickened and pushed into 1976, where reauthorization failed, and into 1977, where it succeeded. One of the principal changes was a significant shift in the balance of policy control. The House achieved a much greater level of control over the shape of air pollution control policy in the reauthorization proceedings. The best evidence for this is that the bill reported out in both 1976 and 1977 by the House Committee on Interstate and Foreign Commerce formed the basis for the amendments agreed upon by House-Senate conferees in both years. This shift in the balance of policy control is significant because the expanded role for the House brought with it renewed and more favorable attention to economic incentive alternatives. Charges received their most favorable and comprehensive consideration, but also their last serious attention in a legislative forum, during these proceedings. Congress in fact incorporated elements of the charge concept in the 1977 legislation. But in laying the new groundwork in 1977, Congress provided for a shift in emphasis away from charges and toward trading schemes and quasi-market arrangements as the principal focus of incentive-based regulatory reform proposals. Congress's action in 1977 also closed off most legislative debate over basic questions about the use of economic incentives in pollution regulation, forcing regulatory reformers in the EPA to dig deep into what Congress had already wrought for legal authority supporting the cause of economic incentives.

Congress's consideration of four provisions, identifiable in some form in both 1976 and 1977 legislation, and finally incorporated into law with the passage of the Clean Air Act Amendments of 1977, provided the primary stimulus for these basic changes in the direction of policy development. All four provisions—the noncompliance penalty, the offset policy, the permit fee provision, and the authorization for studies on economic incentive alternatives—in some way address the use of incentives and the arguments in their favor put forth by economists. The reasons for development of each provision and the supporting and opposing arguments reveal the evolution after 1975 of congressional opinion about the use of incentives to control pollution.

The noncompliance penalty, modeled in part on the Connecticut Plan, became section 120 of the amended Clean Air Act (91 Stat. 715). The Senate called its version of the provision the "delayed compliance penalty." In an attempt to reflect more closely a true emission charge, the House originally referred to this provision as the "excess emission fee" in 1976. In the 1977 bill the committee changed the provision to its present title in the statute.

It is quite clear that, despite the repeated reference to arguments favoring the "economic approach" in committee reports, the primary purpose of this provision was to rectify poor compliance records accumulated by many industries under the existing legislation, and to provide an enforcement device with teeth. A consideration of incentives *per se* and the importance of internalizing the cost of pollution were important but secondary objectives. For example, the Senate, with identical language in both 1976 and 1977 committee reports, stressed that the penalty was meant as "an effort to assure effective and fair implementation of the requirement that compliance with emission limitations be achieved... while providing a balanced, economic disincentive to delay" (U.S. Senate 1976: 38). Hence, the Senate emphasized effective, fair enforcement; the economic disincentive was more important for providing *balance* in application of the law than it was for making the law more effective in the economic sense of harnessing self-interest. The Senate's special concern was with economic advantages of noncompliance like unfair competition, and thus difficulties in enforcement.

The House committee reports in both years provided the same elaborate treatise on the problems of the "regulatory" approach, on the economics of pollution, and on the advantages of the incentive approach. The following excerpt is indicative of that discussion.

The 1970 Clean Air Act based its strategy for air pollution control almost exclusively on a regulatory model. . . . Absent adequate penalties for noncompliance (or other economic incentives), the act did not contain adequate measures to assure the internalization of environmental costs by the businesses or enterprises that were emitting air pollutants. . . .

When the price of any pollution generating product is not required to include the costs of pollution abatement, there is no marketplace incentive for development of nonpolluting production processes and methods. (U.S. House 1977: 72–73)

Nevertheless, the primary concern of the House was also with the problem of enforcement. "The limited nature of... enforcement options has undermined the credibility of enforcement efforts under the act. . . . " (U.S. House 1977: 72). Hence, the objectives of the noncompliance penalty were first to remedy the enforcement shortcomings of the regulatory approach and second to assure a greater degree of internalization of the costs of air pollution (U.S. House 1977: 75).

It is not clear how well House members understood the concept of economic incentives. The lengthy discussions on it in the committee reports most likely reflect the arguments of committee staff. Nevertheless, the effort at understanding was there and many key advantages of incentives were listed and discussed. Further, the committee demonstrated at least some recognition of the difficulties of actually designing an emission charge system by noting that the noncompliance penalty fell far short of a true charge system and was in fact a hybrid of the charge system and the regulatory approach (U.S. House 1976: 59). But most important, the values of efficiency and cost-effectiveness, the hallmarks of the economic incentive approach, took a backseat in the minds of congressmen to concerns about fair, effective enforcement. Representatives saw incentives as, at best, one means toward those ends, but not to the point of dispensing with the "regulatory" approach.

As for objections to the provision, they were few and relatively mild, yet instructive of congressional thinking on this subject. In 1976, House critics charged that the excess emission fee was unfair and inequitable because it gave the EPA administrator too much discretion, allowing the administrator to serve as "prosecutor, judge, and jury in determining guilt and assessing the penalty" (U.S. House 1976: 461). Critics also considered the fee strictly punitive, not offering firms any real incentive to invest in compliance, and redundant of other compliance provisions in the legislation. Finally, some House members attacked the noncompliance penalty as too rigid and inflexible, which is often cited by advocates of incentives as an advantage, in that polluters cannot then escape the charge through special pleading.

The offset policy became Part D of Title I of the Clean Air Act (91 Stat. 746), entitled "Plan Requirements for Nonattainment Areas." The historical development of offsets or "tradeoffs" is rather convoluted and will be given only brief treatment here, with a more detailed discussion presented in chapter 4 (also see Liroff 1980). The stimulus for the development of the offset provision appears to have had little if anything to do with a desire to incorporate incentives into the air pollution regulatory apparatus. The concern of both legislators and regulators was with the so-called "growth ban" in the Clean Air Act. Areas of the country not "attaining" all the NAAQS by the mandated deadlines would not be permitted to accept new or substantially expanded existing sources of pollution that would add to emissions already exceeding one or more of the standards. Not surprisingly, an environmental law preventing economic growth in numerous areas of the country, especially major urban areas experiencing economic decline, was a political hot potato no one wanted to handle. Regulators and legislators scrambled to find ways around the growth ban. The Ford administration proposed legislation to deal with the problem. This proposal became the provision in the Senate bill to address the growth ban, and was dubbed the "steel amendment" because among other things it addressed the expansion needs of U.S. steel companies with facilities in nonattainment areas.

The 1976 report accompanying the Senate bill reported out of the Committee on Public Works identified the purposes of the provision as providing "an *exception* to allow *greater flexibility* in the administration of the Act and *opportunity for growth* of national industrial capability" (U.S. Senate 1976: 42, emphasis added). The House Committee on Interstate and Foreign Commerce report of the same year identified the objective of the provision as reconciling the conflicting concerns of public health and the harmful economic impact of a growth ban. Neither the House nor Senate bills in 1976 actually provided for offsets. Instead, the House provided a "variance" for industrial expansion and new economic growth. The Senate stipulated that "combined emissions from the existing and new facilities be sufficiently less than the previous total of all emissions from the site to represent reasonable further progress toward attainment . . . " (U.S. Senate 1976: 43). The term "offset" and the requirement that there be offsetting emissions between new and existing sources appeared in the 1977 legislation in response to action by the EPA administrator at the end of 1976, when he issued an "Interpretative Ruling" for emission offsets as a way to get around the growth ban in the Clean Air Act (U.S. EPA 1976). Congress accepted the EPA action and incorporated it into law with some modifications.

The offset policy was an immediate administrative and legislative response to a critical flaw in a major public policy. One would have to stretch the facts beyond any measure of reasonableness to argue that an attempt to incorporate economic incentives into air pollution control law was part of the original impetus behind the offset policy. The *impact* of the offset provision was something else entirely, however, because it did more to stimulate the expansion of programmatic initiatives using economic incentives than all three other incentive-oriented provisions in the 1977 amendments combined. The offset policy provided a window of opportunity, albeit initially a narrowly opened one, allowing EPA reformers room to maneuver in exploring alternative control strategies with at least the semblance of incentive characteristics. Furthermore, it turned the attention of policy makers and regulators away from a dominant focus on charges and legitimized program initiatives utilizing trading and quasi-market schemes.

The timing of the "growth ban" crisis and the rise of the offset idea was also propitious. The offset policy became law with a new administration settling into place. President Carter expressed a strong desire to improve the efficiency and cost-effectiveness of federal programs. His administration placed into many regulatory agencies, including EPA, personnel who were interested in trying out new techniques, including those based on the economic approach. As subsequent chapters will show, the offset policy became a critical instrument toward such ends.

Objections raised to the offset provision were consistent between the House and Senate. Critics charged that offsets were unworkable for the following reasons: (1) offsets made pollution a marketable commodity and thus inequitably benefitted those firms that had poor compliance records because such firms had more emissions to "sell" (In other words, the policy "pays off polluters" [U.S. Senate 1977b: 111]. These critics clearly foresaw the impact offsets would have on air pollution regulatory policy); (2) offsets were inequitable because they applied only to major (100 + tons per year) polluters. Hence, slightly smaller polluters could skirt the requirements, and many other firms would have the incentive to reduce their emissions just enough to avoid the provision as well; (3) offsets were inequitable because only very large, wealthy firms could afford to mount the effort necessary to convince other firms to reduce emissions enough to obtain offsets; and (4) the offset provision was just a numbers game that evaded the tough question of environmental quality versus economic growth posed by the Clean Air Act.

The remaining two provisions need be addressed only briefly. The permit fee was exclusively a House initiative and was listed under the heading "Internalization of Cost" in the 1977 House committee report (U.S. House 1977: 217). The purposes of the provision were: (1) to provide states a mechanism for generating funds to cover budget shortfalls experienced in implementing the Clean Air Act; and (2) to "assure that the costs of the permit program be internalized in the operating costs of polluting businesses. This in turn should create further incentive for the development of nonpolluting processes that would not require a permit." The House committee discussion of the provision was short and, without public objection, was incorporated into the law as section 110(a)(2)(K) of the Clean Air Act (91 Stat. 694).

The statutory provision mandating reports on economic incentive alternatives was also a House committee initiative. The committee justified the reports by drawing on the same discussion surrounding the noncompliance penalty. The mandate was incorporated as section 405 of the act, which directed the EPA, the Council on Environmental Quality, and the Council of Economic Advisors to undertake a study of economic measures that could "provide incentives to abate air pollution to a greater degree than is required under existing provisions of the Clean Air Act (and regulations thereunder) . . . " (91 Stat. 794).

It is the enduring irony of the attention Congress directed toward incentives in 1976 and 1977 that the legislation the lawmakers enacted is almost universally considered a monumental example of regulation by command and control. Equally ironic is the impact the provisions in the legislation clearly inspired by economic incentive ideas have had: no record of the EPA administrator ever assessing a noncompliance penalty exists; no evidence of any state ever assessing permit fees under that provision of the act has come to light; and reports prepared under the section 405 mandate have generated little interest among incentive advocates and policy makers despite findings very favorable to both charge and marketable permit schemes (U.S. CEQ 1979). It is only the offset policy, with the shakiest "incentive-based rationale" behind it, that has had a lasting impact on the development of regulatory policies incorporating economic incentives. From 1970–1977, then, open opposition to incentives, expressed in the early years most vocally in the Senate, had evolved into rhetorical support for economic incentive ideas in congressional action dominated by the House. Such support was not sufficient, however, to transform rhetoric into statutory authority. Congressmen had become, at best, ambivalent about the use of economic incentives when thinking about pollution policy. When the time for action arrived, however, command and control carried the day.

The Shift from Legislative to Administrative Attention:
1977–1982

Even before the 1977 legislation left Congress, Senators Gary Hart (D–CO) and Edmund Muskie engaged in a brief debate on the merits of charge schemes during hearings reviewing the status of EPA programs just prior to the change in administrations. Senator Hart had emerged as a champion of charge schemes and defended them in this forum on the following grounds: (1) they might be easier to implement than a regulatory system; and (2) they are less burdensome, intrusive, stifling, complicated, and probably require less bureaucracy. Senator Muskie reiterated counterarguments he raised in 1972: (1) charge schemes had not been proved through actual use; and (2) more rather than less bureaucracy would be needed; it would just be a different kind of bureaucracy, pursuing different objectives. Muskie also raised the new argument that the incentive of a charge scheme would not lead to clean up but to change in consumer preferences in favor of products in which the costs of pollution are not internalized and hence the product is cheaper. In other words, Muskie was expressing the view that the market might be too uncertain a device to rely on in trying to clean up pollution. He wondered aloud what perverse outcomes the market as a policy tool might bring about (U.S. Senate 1977a).

Save for one episode, the four years between the passage of the 1977 amendments and 1981, when Congress's interest in EPA's implementation of the offset provision and in the agency's growing work on incentive schemes perked up, the public record is barren of anything worthy of analysis regarding congressional consideration of economic incentives. After the bruising battles of 1976 and 1977, and with legislative provisions recognizing, however minimally in terms of policy effect, the potential merits of economic incentives in aiding pollution control, Congress appeared in no mood to tamper further with the framework it had established in 1970.

The single interesting episode occurred in 1979, during oversight hearings on the Clean Air Act in the House. Congressman William Dannemeyer (R–CA) again raised the question of taxing pollution rather than "trying to regulate it out of our society" (U.S. House 1979: 165). Dannemeyer argued that the advantage of pollution taxes was that "we will get less of it [pollution] because it is in the interest, the economic interest of the polluters, to so adjust their industrial lives and otherwise avoid the tax." Two state agency officials testifying before the House panel at the time of Dannemeyer's comments suggested that Congress had attempted to do that with the noncompliance penalty. They were ignored. However, Lewis Perl of National Economic Research Associates took Dannemeyer's comments to heart as he testified in favor of yet another pollution tax proposal. Perl listed the following benefits of his proposal:

1. It would effectively eliminate those cases in which the cost of emissions control vastly exceeds the accepted social estimates of benefits. Presumably people would spend on controls up to the point where the marginal expenditure equalled the tax and not beyond that level.

2. It would eliminate those cases in which a given level of control could be achieved more cheaply by the distribution of the controls among the sources.

3. It would eliminate the inherent conflict between emission controls and economic growth. (U.S. House 1979: 209–210)

Perl attacked the "burdens and inefficiencies of the current scheme" and Dannemeyer pronounced Perl's proposal "a good idea." No further discussion of the concept took place, however.

Both the House and the Senate held Clean Air Act reauthorization hearings in 1981. The offset provision in the 1977 amendments was the focus of extensive testimony from state and local officials, industry representatives, and environmentalists, and considerable discussion among witnesses and committee members in both the House and Senate ensued. In addition, the Senate Committee on Environment and Public Works devoted the entire morning of one day of hearings exclusively to the subject of "controlled trading of emission rights," the immediate precursor of the emissions trading program.

The offset policy was clearly the source of substantial exchange of views at both sets of hearings because it was a legislative provision. Witnesses at the two sets of hearings both villified and commended the idea. Those on the attack argued that the offset provision was "burdensome," a "significant disincentive to locating new plants" in urban areas, and it "had nothing to do with reducing emissions" (U.S. House 1981: 25, 41–42). Those on the defensive argued that the offset provision was a "quite logical and workable way" to achieve attainment of air quality standards in nonattainment areas (U.S. House 1981: 16).

House and Senate committee members responded to this conflicting testimony largely with two kinds of questions: (1) questions about tinkering with the offset provision to improve it; and (2) questions about special cases, such as control of hazardous air pollutants, where offsets might be useful or, in the other extreme, their use should be explicitly ruled out. The character of the lawmakers' questions and their dialogue with witnesses reinforces the assessment made earlier, that Congress did not perceive the offset provision as an economic incentive device. The congressional view might instead be interpreted as defining the offset provision as an appropriately innovative extension of command and control, but that limits had to be placed on its use because of the greater uncertainty in the control of pollution sources manifested by the use of offsets.

The principal witnesses in the Senate's review of EPA efforts in devel-

oping incentive-based programs were Phillip Reed of the Environmental
Law Institute and William Drayton, by then a private consultant, but for-
merly an EPA assistant administrator directly responsible for the programs
that would eventually become emissions trading. These two gentlemen
presented extensive prepared testimony detailing the relative advantages of
command and control and incentive-based regulation (U.S. Senate 1981).
They also detailed the merits of "bubbles" and "controlled trading of emission rights" (see chapter 4).

Yet the senators on the committee expressed little substantive interest in
the ideas discussed by Reed and Drayton. Moreover, no legislative response
to these hearings has appeared or is likely to appear. Congress has yet to
reauthorize the Clean Air Act, a step that is now five years overdue, but a
legislative position on economic incentives in any reauthorized Clean Air
Act was mapped out in 1983, although it may no longer be in force. At
that time, congressional staff interviewed for this study insisted that no
version of a bill to reauthorize the Clean Air Act would contain any explicit
references to trading schemes and other incentive-based reforms of the air
pollution regulatory system. Committee aids identified various reasons for
this position, including that some lawmakers did not consider it necessary
to endorse administrative actions in the law, while others disliked incentive
approaches and vehemently opposed legislative endorsement of their use.
Most importantly, however, both House and Senate committees seemed,
at most, only willing to consider pilots or experiments of incentive-based
programs so that evidence could be assembled on whether they really work.

Two things are therefore especially striking about the 1981 hearings. First,
they are largely devoid of any dialogue and debate about the relative merits
of command and control versus economic incentives among senators and
representatives, in clear contrast to most of the hearings that took place
through 1977. The subject of incentives in the post–1977 hearings arose
largely because EPA was developing program options using incentive techniques. Hence the lawmakers' attention was concentrated on oversight of
administrative action rather than on the merits of policy alternatives. Second, the hearings record and the comments of committee staff strongly
suggest that Congress had reached a stable position on economic incentives
in air pollution control. In essence, the use of incentives Congress endorsed
in 1977 (that is, in areas where no significant policy impacts were likely)
was as far as it was willing to go. Any further development of incentive-
based regulatory alternatives was thereafter to be an administrative matter,
to be explored within existing statutory limits.

POLITICS, LEGISLATOR PREFERENCES, AND CONGRESSIONAL SUPPORT FOR COMMAND AND CONTROL

Scholars and EPA officials continue to debate whether unambiguous legislative action supporting incentive-based regulatory programs for air pol-

lution control is needed to bring such programs fully to life. The prospects for such congressional action appear slim. Over nearly 20 years of intense effort to develop an acceptable regulatory structure for air pollution control, Congress has staked out a position that places no significant statutory authority behind efforts to use economic incentives to regulate air pollution. Despite the rhetoric of 1976 and 1977, the record from 15 years of legislative consideration of economic incentives and the explicit regulatory structure designed into the Clean Air Act clearly signal steadfast congressional preference for command and control. Questions about why Congress has come down strongly on the side of command and control in the face of a barrage of criticisms of that approach, and in the face of the continued stream of rhetorical support for incentive-based regulation, from academic analysts, administrative officials, and even some lawmakers, have attracted the attention of scholars interested in regulatory design and the politics of legislative decisions about regulatory form. Various answers to this conundrum, examined in light of the evidence from the public record, will serve to round out this exploration of the legislative background behind emissions trading and the politics of regulatory reform in the EPA.

Five explanations for Congress's failure to fully endorse in law the use of economic incentives to control air pollution have received some measure of acceptance by students of regulatory politics. The first of these may be called the "technical complexity" argument, as advanced, for example, by Kneese and Schultze (1975), who contend that the policy demands on Congress have changed substantially from an earlier era. No longer can Congress merely decide *what* the federal government must do to respond to some significant social policy issue. Now Congress must also decide *how* the job should be done. That is, Congress must become actively involved in designing, in some detail, policy instruments.[3]

Kneese and Schultze argue, however, that Congress has neither the capacity nor the supporting facilities and resources to undertake such a demanding task—to develop and evaluate in adequate detail, that is, a wide array of alternative solutions to problems of social regulation. Given these deficiencies, Congress either does a poor job of developing and evaluating alternative policy instruments, or it delegates the task to administrative agencies without sufficient understanding of the legal authority the agencies need to complete the task successfully.

Morris Fiorina finds much to question in the technical complexity argument. "Congress has chosen to legislate any number of seemingly complex issues. Where the incentive exists, legislators find the time and resources to deal with complexity" (Fiorina 1985: 185). Fiorina further suggests that a second reason, "to doubt the complexity explanation . . . arises from an honest look at the ability of the administrative system to deal with complexity" (1985: 185). Fiorina asks, "Is it not conceivable that augmented congressional staffs could deal with complex issues as competently as and perhaps considerably faster than executive or independent agencies?" (1985: 185).

The evidence from the legislative history of the Clean Air Act amendments of 1970 and 1977 is strongly supportive of Fiorina's arguments against technical complexity as a barrier to congressional consideration of alternative policy instruments. As Jones (1975) and Marcus (1980b) effectively argue, strong pressure from public interest groups, and public opinion generally, presented senators and representatives with ample political incentives to confront the legally and technically complex problem of regulating air pollution.

In addition, the competency of the administrative system to tackle the problem was at best questionable because no administrative system with sufficient resources and experience in fact existed that could address the problem to the extent demanded by the political system. EPA was only authorized and organized simultaneously with the passage of the 1970 amendments. Preexisting bureaucratic units responsible for pollution control at the time were only loosely associated, and together they had little experience in undertaking a massive program of pollution abatement and air quality control. With little start-up time and inadequate resources, EPA effectively failed in the admittedly unreasonable mission given it by Congress when so many states missed the original statutory deadlines for attainment of all the ambient standards. Even after the EPA was fully operative, it was Congress that again faced the political pressure and found the time and resources required for a further assault on the complex problem of air pollution control, culminating in the 1977 amendments.

Finally, the public record shows that Congress undertook a reasonably complete exploration of the arguments for and against alternative regulatory approaches to air pollution control in hearings, floor debate, and committee staff work. Congress's failure fully to endorse incentive schemes in legislated solutions to the problem of air pollution control cannot reasonably be explained by congressional ignorance about alternative policy instruments like economic incentives.

Kneese and Schultze (1975) also advance a second explanation, what might be called the "discipline bias" argument, to explain Congress's reluctance to use markets and the price system as regulatory instruments. They contend that because the majority of the nation's lawmakers are lawyers, Congress tends to rely on "old tried (if not true) remedies" (Kneese and Schultze 1975: 116), emphasizing direct regulation and subsidies. As Kneese and Schultze state, "the fact that the incentive approach is often given such short shrift in favor of the regulatory approach is hardly unexpected in view of the predominance of lawyers in Congress" (Kneese and Schultze 1975: 116–117).

The public record clearly does not support the notion that Congress gave incentive-based regulatory alternatives short shrift in its deliberations on air pollution control. Furthermore, the lawmakers went beyond mere deliberation and incorporated incentive ideas into the 1977 amendments, if only in the form of very limited, largely toothless provisions. The offset policy stands out of course, but it has very dubious origins in an economic incentives rationale.

That Congress continued to prefer command and control after a reasonably thorough ventilating of the arguments for and against incentive-based alternatives might be explained at least partially by the legal orientation of many members, however. As Kneese and Schultze explain, legal training and legal reasoning emphasize changing social behavior by changing how rights and duties are specified. The economic approach, on the other hand, emphasizes modifying incentives in the marketplace that induce people to act in certain ways because of self-interest. Congress clearly paid considerable attention to the rights of citizens and the duties of polluters in structuring air pollution regulation. Yet what congressmen said on the record, in hearings, in floor debate, and in legislative conferences strongly indicates that their concerns about the problem of air pollution control and the role the market and economic incentives might play in the design of an effective remedy are more closely associated with their role as democratically elected legislators rather than lawyers. This argument is explored more fully below, in assessing the merits of a "conflict and uncertainty" explanation for congressional reticence toward incentive schemes.

Yet a third explanation for Congress's refusal to incorporate economic incentive techniques fully into the air pollution regulatory structure is the "vested interest" argument. This argument states simply that the adoption of incentive schemes is politically unfeasible because of opposition from legislators who are committed to the present scheme of direct regulation (Marcus 1980b: 17, 171). Key senators and representatives have a vested interest in what they have wrought. Further, legislators who support economic incentive ideas find it too costly in political resources to try to overcome this opposition. As Marcus explains, crucial actors like Edmund Muskie in the Senate and Henry Waxman (D-CA) in the House rejected the incentive approach because "the adoption of new schemes would be interpreted as a failure of programs they helped author" (Marcus 1982: 181).

Related to the vested interest argument in ascribing to legislators a strong sense of political self-interest is the "shift-the-responsibility" argument. This argument contends that congressmen prefer to shift the responsibility for making tough regulatory decisions, including both the investigation of alternative means and the imposition of the costs of regulation, onto the bureaucracy. Michael Hayes (1978: 149–154) has described this process with respect to regulatory policies generally, and Morris Fiorina (1985) has reinforced and extended the argument. Leonard Lane has expressed the shift-the-responsibility argument succinctly for the case of pollution control. "A regulatory solution allows the legislator to satisfy his constituents by voting for a 'tough' law. At the same time he can feel assurance that however rigorous the legislation appears to be, the regulators are unlikely to impose anything 'unreasonable' on a politically powerful industry" (Lane 1977: 683). This matches quite well with Fiorina's (1985: 187–193) interpretation of the argument, in which a legislator seeks the most beneficial trade-off between the loss in his ability to claim credit for benefits delivered to constituents and the gain in his ability to shift the blame for costs imposed by policies onto the regulatory agency.

Introspection and casual observation provide at least partial substantiation for both the "vested interest" and "shift-the-responsibility" arguments. Human nature seems to include the desire to avoid conflict, to claim credit but shift blame, and to defend mightily things to which one has made major contributions. No confirmation that these are the principal motive forces behind Congress's refusal to incorporate incentive schemes more fully into law can be found in the public record, but it would of course be foolish to search for such confirmation. No politician worth his salt would explain publicly that he was making a particular policy decision because he had a strong personal investment in the status quo, or that he did not wish to confront the tough questions, or that he preferred to displace blame for the potential future failure of a policy onto someone else's shoulders. Although no disconfirmation of these two arguments is apparent in the evidence at hand, that should not prevent a continued search for broader, more fundamental reasons behind Congress's choice of command and control to the near exclusion of incentive-based alternatives in structuring the regulation of air pollution. Moreover, that societal values and norms tend strongly to denigrate the actions of politicians motivated by self-interest or cowardice suggests that at least some politicians may act in response to loftier, more "publicly interested" motives.

Consider, then, a final explanation: the "conflict and uncertainty" argument. As Matthew McCubbins describes the conflict and uncertainty argument, "Congress will prefer the imposition of command and control instruments for the implementation of its policy objectives. . . . When there is more conflict and greater uncertainty, congressmen have greater concern with procedural safeguards. The very flexibility of economic incentives (the source of their strength to economists) is interpreted as uncontrolled uncertainty" (McCubbins 1985: 743).

Conflict and uncertainty clearly characterized the political process that produced the nation's air pollution control system. The politics of air pollution control were (and are) rife with conflict among environmentalists, consumers, public interest lobbies, industries, and states and cities. And the policy formulation process for air pollution regulation obviously proceeded from a base of uncertainty. Neither legislators nor administrators at the time had any experience in undertaking far reaching environmental cleanup and control actions. Thus was spawned Jones's (1975) speculative augmentation of policy. Further, as Senator Muskie observed in 1977, "It is appealing on its face, you know, that you make people pay when they pollute for failure to clean up. But, on the other hand, we operate in a profit-motivated society and economy, and the temptation is simply to pass those costs along to the consumer and let him apply the discipline either to the regulators or to the manufacturers. . . . You know, that is an uncertain kind of aim" (Senate 1977a: 43). The greater uncertainty in control engendered in the offset policy was also a cause of concern among a number of representatives and senators, as the objections to that policy cited previously clearly attest.

Yet the conflict and uncertainty argument can only go so far in explaining the actions of Congress since 1970 with respect to the use of economic incentives in pollution regulation. In the midst of a highly conflictual policy issue, Congress was clearly uncertain about what policy instruments would prove most effective in cleaning up a nation's air fouled by pollutants. The evidence from floor debates, hearings, and committee reports shows, however, that many senators and representatives had legitimate, well-defined preferences with respect to the nature of political institutions, priorities among competing societal values, and the usefulness of the market to achieve broad public aims that guided them in their policy deliberations. As hinted at earlier, these are preferences one might more closely associate with legislators as democratic politicians than with legislators as lawyers or other professionals. It is in the political arena, after all, where one not only has the exclusive opportunity to pursue broad goals inspired by some notion of the public interest, but where one is *expected* to serve the public interest, however ill-defined that concept may be. That is the role society expects politicians to fulfill. How they define the public interest will follow from basic preferences they hold, but those preferences are surely shaped by their social role.

In the case of concerns about political institutions, for example, the public record shows former House Ways and Means Committee Chairman Wilbur Mills expressing a strong distrust of uses of the tax code for objectives, like social and economic regulation, other than raising revenue. This does not mean that Congress does not use the tax code for other purposes. Clearly it does, in redistributing wealth and protecting declining vital industries through tax "benefits," for example. But Mills's position clearly indicates that a legislator's preferences for the structure and character of a key political institution like the tax system may guide his choice of policy. Another example of this same type of concern is Senator Muskie's repeated point that incentive schemes would require multiple bureaucracies, with potentially conflicting objectives, overseeing the implementation of environmental laws.

The evidence also indicates that the problem of reconciling competing values was clearly on the minds of legislators in the decision-making process leading up to the passage of the 1977 amendments. Both House and Senate committee members gave considerable attention to efficiency and cost-effectiveness as values deserving consideration. However, the lawmakers kept these values subordinate to others, especially equity, fairness, and effectiveness of enforcement.

Finally, to make emphatic the possible link between role and preferences as the basis of Congress's rejection of all but a very limited position for economic incentives in pollution regulation, one need look no further than Senator Baker's observation about human nature. As the Senator from Tennessee observed, people do not respond only to laws that touch their economic self-interest, the "internal revenue code" as he put it. Individuals will also respond, Baker implied, to laws that legitimately command fulfillment of important duties and obligations. Many legislators therefore reject the use of the market as an overt policy tool precisely because it fails to encourage such behavior (see Kelman 1981).

It is of course quite risky to take the public utterances of politicians at face value. In the end, the vested interests of politicians and their desire to avoid conflict and shift blame for the costs of policy decisions may fully explain the actions of Congress in the issue at hand. Nonetheless, if the public record is at all indicative of the thinking that was behind Congress's overwhelming choice of command and control to regulate air pollution, then one may reasonably conclude that such policy thinking was anchored in the desires of lawmakers to serve varying, perhaps self-defined, conceptions of the public interest that emphasize particular types of institutions as the bedrock of social and political organization.

CONCLUSION

Rhetorical support for incentive schemes is clearly evident in the legislative history of the Clean Air Act amendments of 1970 and 1977. In the end, however, Congress placed little statutory authority behind efforts to employ incentive-based approaches for regulating pollution. It chose instead to place almost exclusive reliance on regulation by directives. Narrow, self-interested motives cannot be ruled out in explaining the actions taken by Congress with regard to incentive schemes. Nevertheless, the public record shows that key lawmakers advanced a number of powerful philosophical arguments against incentive-based regulation. Those arguments, including deep-seated concerns about possible bureaucratic goal conflict, prioritizing prominent yet competing societal values, and the desire of lawmakers generally to serve what they define as the public interest, deserve greater attention in research on legislative choice of regulatory forms.

Of greater importance to the issue at hand, the minimal statutory acknowledgment Congress did give to the economic incentive approach, combined with the circumscribed administrative discretion embodied in a legally, administratively, and technically complex but flawed public law, gave the EPA little flexibility to explore, within the basic command-and-control structure of the Clean Air Act, administrative options for regulatory reform principally focused on incentive schemes. It is to the primary subject of EPA development of incentive-based reforms of air pollution control in the face of statutory limitations, to the origins of emissions trading, and to the organizational change elements embodied in the agency's regulatory reform efforts, that the study now turns.

NOTES

1. Congress originally specified five criteria pollutants: sulfur oxides, particulate matter, carbon monoxide, hydrocarbons, and photochemical oxidants. Subsequent research and legal reviews produced a list of seven pollutants. The more narrow designation of ozone replaces photochemical oxidants, and nitrogen oxides and lead now appear on the list.

2. This provision spawned a few state experiments in alternative emission control strategies with features similar to bubbles and offsets, important program components of emissions trading. However, this state activity appears to have had little bearing on the development of the various programs central to the efforts of the regulatory reformers at EPA headquarters, as described in more detail in chapter 4.

3. Ackerman and Hassler's (1981) study of the politics surrounding the development of the 1977 amendments to the Clean Air Act and the controversy over "forced scrubbing" provides a searching critique of what happens when Congress goes beyond legislating and gets extensively involved in dictating administrative actions. An expanded discussion of their argument can be found in chapter 7.

4

AN EMISSIONS TRADING CHRONICLE

Every public organization has a distinctive character. The features that distinguish one administrative agency from another encompass far more than agency missions and political fortunes. Organizational character embraces the symbols, ideals, norms, values, ideas, and moral tone that permeate activity within a bureaucracy. Many of these qualities are captured in terms such as "organizational culture" or "governing ethos." What Gareth Morgan describes as corporate culture is equally applicable to public organizations.

Organizations are mini-societies that have their own distinctive patterns of culture and subculture. Thus one organization may see itself as a tight-knit team or family that believes in working together. Another... may be highly fragmented, divided into groups that think about the world in very different ways, or that have different aspirations as to what their organization should be. Such patterns of belief or shared meaning, fragmented or integrated, and supported by various operating norms and rituals, can exert a decisive influence on the overall ability of the organization to deal with the challenges it faces. (Morgan 1986: 121)

One of the most potent forces for shaping the distinctive character of an administrative agency is the ideology of the dominant profession represented among agency personnel.[1] As Steven Kelman has observed in his research on the Occupational Safety and Health Administration (OSHA), "the most important factor explaining OSHA decisions on the content of regulations has been the pro-protectionist values of agency officials, derived from the ideology of the safety and health professional and the organizational mission of OSHA" (Kelman 1980: 250).

The ideology of an agency's dominant professional personnel can mold organizational culture or the ethos of the agency by defining what is most relevant to the conduct of agency business, including everything from office politics to formal policy deliberations. As Robert Bell has observed, "Culture normally refers to the realm of ideals, ideas, and symbols, and the term therefore captures . . . the understanding administrators share about what kind of talk is relevant and persuasive in policy discussions" (Bell 1985: 4).

William Ruckleshaus, the Environmental Protection Agency's first administrator, contributed greatly to the establishment of what can best be called a "culture of enforcement" when he took command of the agency in its very first days. The organizational character Ruckleshaus helped to shape was heavily oriented toward legal reasoning, activism, and an interventionist role for the EPA, and it guided policy decisions within the agency through the end of the Ford administration. Attorneys were the dominant professionals in the agency (Ruckleshaus was a Justice Department attorney before he became EPA administrator). Environmental engineers, especially from EPA's predecessor agencies, principally the Federal Water Quality Administration and the National Air Pollution Control Administration, also contributed to the cultivation of an enforcement culture in the agency.

The organizational ethos that emerged from this professional core stressed vigorous regulation of pollutants, engineering standards as the most effective way to control pollution, and regulation as an adversarial process (Meier 1985: 163). Alfred Marcus explains the rationale behind the establishment of this governing ethos favored by Ruckleshaus. "In order to establish credibility with environmental groups, Ruckleshaus believed that the agency had to cultivate an "activist image" and had to acquire the reputation of being a vigorous enforcer of pollution control laws" (Marcus 1980b: 90).

Given the potential for the ideology of the dominant profession in an agency to shape that agency's bureaucratic character, a fascinating question arises: what happens when another profession, whose ideology would lead it to shape the organizational culture of a public bureaucracy in contrasting or even antithetical ways, begins to gain prominence in an agency?

A dominant professional ethos or organizational culture does not give way easily, of course. Agency personnel, temporary political appointees and career civil servants alike, who sculptured an agency's original professional identity, or who are otherwise committed to the tenets of the organizational culture established at the agency's founding, and thus share a common view of the agency's mission as well as a broader view of the world, can prove to be powerful foils for attempts to change the way a public organization goes about its business. James Q. Wilson has made this point even more forcefully. "Few organizations . . . can tolerate having more than a single governing ethos: the need for morale, for a sense of mission and of distinctive competence, and for standard operating procedures means that competing norms will be suppressed, ignored, or isolated" (Wilson 1973: 162).

When a group of professionals, with only limited previous influence over agency business, begins to gain prominence in an agency, the professional ideology that challenges agency orthodoxy may indeed be suppressed. Suppose, however, that the professional ideology and the new organizational ethos it champions are in some way irrepressible, perhaps because they are part of a broader movement for policy reform with powerful allies outside the organization. One then is likely to see highly divisive issues and controversies dominating policy deliberations about reform programs. Ideas become the principal weapons of policy discourse under such circumstances, with the antagonists making exhortations to basic ideals and symbols of broad-based values in defending their positions.

In the case of the EPA at its inception, Wilson's argument seems irrefutable. Economic incentives as alternative regulatory options, at least in the form of effluent charges, had been under consideration in the executive branch for some years before EPA came into being in December 1970 (a scant two weeks before Congress passed the 1970 Clean Air Act amendments). Yet the dominant enforcement culture within the agency acted to suppress most attempts to apply economic incentive ideas to EPA's regulatory programs. Wilson offers his own interpretation of the circumstances.

In the precarious early months of the EPA, when environmentalists were expressing skepticism about the Nixon administration's commitment to environmental programs, any sign that EPA was even considering effluent charges would have immediately been interpreted as an indication that the agency proposed to "sell licenses to pollute." Such a charge, however misleading, would have dealt a serious blow to the EPA's need to find some political breathing room. (Wilson 1980: 376)

Marcus in turn has argued that strategies for using economic incentive schemes in EPA's regulatory programs failed to develop because of obstacles outside the agency, especially political opposition in Congress. He argues that after 1977, the agency "grafted economic incentives in an incremental and piecemeal fashion on an existing directive framework" (Marcus 1980b: 171).

The source of advocacy for economic incentives within EPA was of course the Office of Planning and Evaluation (later the Office of Planning and Management—OPM), the unit Ruckleshaus created and staffed with economists to help him deal with the pressures placed on the agency by the Quality of Life Review. Although the economists in OPM were in charge of running the agency's regulatory review process, which meant for the most part examining regulatory alternatives and recommending the least costly options (Marcus 1980a: 289), their influence over the forms of regulation EPA chose to use remained limited so long as the policy preferences of lawyers and engineers drove policy making in the agency.

Thus the story of regulatory reform inside the Environmental Protection Agency is indeed, at least in the beginning, the story of incremental and piecemeal policy change. It is also the story of key decision makers in the agency finding the necessary political breathing room to pursue change through creative interpretation of a tightly drawn pollution control statute. After 1977, especially from 1978 to 1982, however, the rise of a major crusade for regulatory reform in the EPA centered around the use of economic incentives is the story of the rise to prominence of OPM's reform-minded policy analysts and their efforts to transform the organizational culture of the agency from one almost completely dominated by legal reasoning and concerns about enforcement to an organizational culture heavily influenced by economic analysis, what might best be described as a "culture of efficiency."

This chapter begins weaving together the threads of that story with an account of the genesis of emissions trading. By way of introduction to this history of the program's development, the chapter begins with a summary of the structure of the policy. The summary is meant to provide a working knowledge of the program that at the same time does not overwhelm the reader with technical detail. The chapter then proceeds with a chronicle of the development of the emissions trading program from its many disparate roots, using documented sources and the interviews with key decision makers undertaken for this study. One purpose of this emissions trading chronicle is to identify the *dramatis personae* in a small but important bureaucratic political drama. A second purpose is to trace the changes in personnel, organization, and political dynamics closely intertwined with the regulatory reform campaign in the agency and the effort to transform its organizational character. The chapter sets the stage for an in-depth examination, in the next two chapters, of the political conflicts engendered by the issues surrounding regulatory reform and the development of emissions trading. The last chapter adds final details to the story, and explores the implications for policy decision making, leadership, and organizational change posed by the movement to reform air pollution regulation in the EPA.

THE FORM AND STRUCTURE OF THE EMISSIONS TRADING PROGRAM

Richard Liroff has observed that understanding the genesis of emissions trading and the political conflicts in the EPA associated with the program's development and implementation is not an easy task. The specialized vocabulary is confusing, and such terms as "bubbles," "netting," "offsets," and "banking" are layered on top of an already complex nomenclature derived from the Clean Air Act (Liroff 1986: 3). Because the present study focuses on the intertwining of internal agency politics and attempts at administrative policy reform, the description of the emissions trading program that follows is meant to provide the reader with only a rudimentary explanation of core concepts and major programmatic elements. More detailed information on the form and structure of the program can be found else-where, especially Liroff (1980 and 1986) and Tietenberg (1985).[2]

Emissions trading is a supplement to the air pollution control program for major stationary sources (for example, manufacturing facilities and power plants). In its comprehensive form, combining offsets, bubbles, banking, and netting, the program most closely resembles a transferable discharge permit (TDP) system (Tietenberg 1985: chapter 2). Emissions trading's claim as incentive-based regulatory reform centers around the program's provisions allowing pollution sources to buy and sell what are called "emission reduction credits" (ERCs) in a manner similar to pollution sources buying and selling discharge permits under a TDP system. Emissions trading represents the synthesis of a number of separate regulatory reform ideas, and four major programmatic elements serve as the corner-stones of the policy's design.

—Emission offsets allow qualified new or expanding pollution sources to operate in areas that have not achieved all emission standards, so-called nonattainment areas, provided the new or modified sources acquire sufficient emission reduction credits from other facilities they own, or from other existing sources in a region, so as to lower actual emissions in the region.

—Bubbles allow existing sources to use emission reduction credits to meet control responsibilities within plants. The policy derives its name from its treatment of multiple emission points in a plant as if they were contained under an imaginary bubble with a single opening in the top. Control requirements are applied not to the multitude of individual emission points but only to the emissions leaving the bubble through the single opening.[3]

—Netting allows emission reduction credits earned elsewhere in a plant to offset the increases expected from expansion or modernization. By meeting the appro-priate tests, a source in either attainment or nonattainment areas may "net out" of administrative and technological requirements, such as preconstruction permits, demanded by the Clean Air Act, by compensating for emission increases generated by expansion and modernization with emission reductions achieved at other points within a facility.

—Banking allows firms to store emission reduction credits for their own future use in bubbles, offsets, or netting. Banking rules also establish regional accounting ledgers or central clearinghouses for emission reduction credits. Firms in search of emission reduction credits that they themselves cannot generate can find other sources with ERC's for the appropriate pollutant through such emission credit banks and trade for or purchase the necessary credits. States operating banks can control and encourage trading, buying, and selling of emission reduction credits between pollution sources through banking rules.

In sum, emission reduction credits are the currency of the emissions trading program, while offsets, bubbles, netting, and banking are the spend-ing rules for the currency (Tietenberg 1985: 7). A pollution source creates an emission reduction credit when it controls an emission point to a greater degree than required to meet legal obligations, and applies to its state control authority for certification of the excess control. Under the provisions of the emissions trading program, to receive certification an emission reduction must be: (1) surplus, (2) enforceable, (3) permanent, and (4) quantifiable.

EPA touts the program as offering pollution sources greater flexibility in the choice of control strategies and thus lower abatement costs than under traditional command and control. The incentives designed into the program encourage sources to change the mix of control technologies envisioned in existing standards, but EPA has attempted to include safeguards in the program[4] to insure that air quality is improved, or at least not adversely affected, by the collective impact of the individual control decisions made by pollution sources. In other words, emissions trading is a policy hybrid, with parts of a market-based approach grafted onto the existing regulatory system for air pollution control.

THE GENESIS OF EMISSIONS TRADING

The public unveiling of EPA's emissions trading program in April 1982 masked the convoluted and controversial path to public policy followed by the reform ideas, some only loosely tied to an economic incentives rationale, embodied in the program. Moreover, as with many public policies, emissions trading has multiple origins, and participants and observers offer varying interpretations of those origins. Milestones in the inception, development, and implementation of emissions trading about which there is some agreement among persons interviewed for this study and among published sources are covered in the history of the program that follows.[5] In addition, the focus is largely on bubbles for existing sources, emission offsets, and banking, with only superficial attention given to other types of bubbles and netting. Emission offsets, banking, and especially existing-source bubbles formed the core of the regulatory reform effort within the agency, and these program components were at the center of the most intense discussion, debate, and political confrontations involving regulatory reform in the EPA.

Early Bubbles and Netting

Scholars and agency personnel agree that the earliest seeds for what would eventually blossom into emissions trading were sown in December 1972 (see Levin 1982: 68; Liroff 1986: 109). At that time the metal smelting industry and the Commerce Department attempted to persuade EPA to expand the definition of "stationary source" in its new source performance standards (NSPS) regulations to include entire plants, rather than discrete points within a plant. The industry objective was to have EPA allow increases at one point in a plant offset decreases at another so that the NSPS requirements for major modifications would not be triggered. In October 1974, EPA first publicly responded to this pressure for change[6] by proposing to alter both the "stationary source" and "modification" definitions in its NSPS regulations. EPA proposed that stationary sources could include "any combination of one or more affected facilities, existing facilities, and facilities to which standards do not apply" (U.S. EPA 1974: 36916). More importantly, EPA proposed that modification would mean there must be an increase in actual emissions. The agency proposed that physical or operational changes to an existing facility could be offset by other changes or improvements to result in no increase in emissions to the atmosphere.

EPA followed its proposed rules 14 months later with final regulations that included the first version of the bubble.[7] The agency described the "bubble concept" as allowing "the trading off of emission increases from one facility undergoing a physical or operational change with emission reductions from another facility, in order to achieve no net increase in the amount of any air pollutant . . . emitted . . . by the stationary source taken as a whole" (U.S. EPA 1975: 58116). The agency resisted efforts to extend the bubble concept to newly constructed facilities, limiting its applicability to modification of existing sources. This first version of an important policy change in air pollution control with mild overtones of the reforms that were to come, but hardly spurred by a "movement" for reform or based on the explicit consideration of alternative, incentive-based regulatory instruments, has come to be labeled both an "applicability bubble" and netting (Liroff 1986: 109), revealing the strong similarities between these two components of emissions trading.[8]

The nature of the political pressure for this policy change, emanating as it did from the combined forces of the Commerce Department and a major industry, is noteworthy. It reveals the extent of the exposure to external political influence the EPA faced both because of its position within the federal executive establishment and because of the Quality of Life Review process and subsequent presidential attempts at regulatory review. Pressure on the EPA from the Commerce Department and the steel industry would later prove to be a key stimulus for the more general movement for regulatory reform in the agency that was to come.

For the time being, however, bubbles in EPA's air pollution regulatory scheme were short-lived. Both environmentalists and industry sued EPA over its 1975 regulations, the former arguing the policy was illegal and the latter arguing the policy was too restrictive. In January 1978, a divided District of Columbia Circuit Court struck down the bubble and the netting concept in ASARCO, Inc. v. EPA (578 F. 2d 319). The court's action was apparently not a cause for great consternation within the agency, however. As Levin notes, "In the two and one-half years this bubble approach had been on the books, not a single plant had tried to use it. The agency had adopted no strategy for *marketing* the reform or *promoting* its use by industries identified as good actors" (Levin 1982: 69, emphasis added).

Levin's observation points out the lack of any internal agency constituency for the bubble concept. The force behind the regulatory changes was solely a focused industry and Commerce Department effort to soften EPA regulations, and when challenged EPA could offer little in the way of a convincing administrative rationale for the changes. EPA's General Counsel in the Carter administration would later make a similar argument.

EPA adopted the 'bubble' only in response to pressure from the smelter industry and the Department of Commerce. . . . [T]here is nothing in the record beyond the most general statements to support the proposition that a 'bubble' is desirable on the merits. (draft letter from Jodie Bernstein to William Nordhaus of the Council of Economic Advisors, quoted in Liroff 1986: 163)

However, a well-defined constituency *against* the bubble existed in EPA offices under the direction of the assistant administrator for air and radiation (Air Programs office), the assistant administrator for enforcement (Enforcement office) (Levin 1982: 68), and among some staff in the Office of General Counsel. This anti-bubble constituency successfully placed limits on the bubble concept out of concern that without such limits the bubble would undermine the objectives of new source performance standards. EPA therefore insisted that the construction of a completely new facility at an existing source meet applicable NSPS regulations regardless of any offsetting emission reductions achieved elsewhere within the source (U.S. EPA 1975: 58416–58417).

Despite the absence of a clearly defined internal agency constituency and the circuit court's neutralization of this redirection in agency policy, the conceptual seeds had been planted for bubbles, netting, and eventually more far reaching, broad-based reform. EPA regulators continued to develop the concepts incrementally, establishing so-called "compliance bubbles"[9] (see Liroff 1986: 110–117), and netting in PSD areas (that is, areas with air quality already meeting all ambient standards). A crisis in implementing the Clean Air Act was looming on the horizon, however, that would overtake these relatively circumscribed[10] policy changes and usher in a true movement for regulatory reform and the accompanying drive to use economic incentives as alternative regulatory instruments.

The Emergence of Emission Offsets and Banking

As the 1975 statutory deadline for attainment of the national ambient air quality standards drew near, EPA began gearing up for the transition from state implementation plans to "air quality maintenance plans" as the basis of the framework for air pollution control. The agency soon realized that it was facing a major administrative and political problem, however, when it discovered that many areas of the country could not attain the national standards by the statutory deadline. Under such circumstances, the Clean Air Act prohibited states from issuing permits for new source construction in nonattainment areas. In response to the emerging administrative and political crisis, the agency undertook to study its patchwork quilt of new source requirements from the perspective of how they would affect growth and development in nonattainment areas. The agency considered a number of new policy options, the principal alternatives being: (1) impose tough sanctions on new growth in nonattainment areas; and (2) allow offsetting emission reductions. The first option was clearly unacceptable politically, so the agency commissioned a number of studies to investigate which industries in critical areas would be affected by nonattainment growth restrictions, and what level of demand and supply of emission offsets could be expected.

The agency gave special attention to the oil and gas industry and the steel industry because many of the facilities in these industries were located in nonattainment areas and relocation was largely precluded by the large economic investments in such existing facilities. Largely independent of EPA, the California Air Resources Board (CARB) was working on a rudimentary offset arrangement with an oil company. Standard Oil of Ohio (SOHIO) planned to build a major new crude oil receiving terminal, for oil from the Alaska pipeline, at Long Beach. The terminal could not be constructed under existing circumstances because the relevant AQCR was not in attainment for the types of pollutants that would be emitted by the terminal. The CARB, the South Coast Air Quality Management District, and SOHIO worked out an agreement whereby SOHIO bought pollution control equipment for a local power plant and guaranteed delivery of low–sulfur fuel oil to the plant so that the new emissions from the terminal would be offset by reduced emissions from the power plant. In 1979, SOHIO abandoned the entire project, citing regulatory burdens (see Liroff 1980: 17–19).

Parallel with the activity in EPA and in California, the congressional committees responsible for reauthorizing the Clean Air Act were also aware of the so-called growth ban in the statute and began to investigate remedies, considering in 1976 amendments to the act providing "exceptions" or "variances" for economic growth in nonattainment areas (see chapter 3). EPA staff shared preliminary information from their studies on the potential for offsets with the committees.

Reauthorization of the Clean Air Act did not pass in 1976 because of a Senate filibuster inspired in part by the "steel amendment" remedy to the Clean Air Act's growth ban, contained in the Senate's version of a reauthorization bill. Faced with the uncertainty, disruption, and political backlash resulting from the lack of a legislative remedy, EPA tried to solve the problem administratively. With only 10 days left in the year, EPA issued its "interpretation" of what the Clean Air Act allowed as far as new source construction in nonattainment areas.[11] The agency argued in its ruling that the law allowed several options, including emission offsets, and defined what an offset entailed. "The principle behind the emission offset is that new sources should be allowed offset credit only for emission reductions from existing sources which would not otherwise be accomplished as a result of the Clean Air Act" (U.S. EPA 1976: 55526). EPA argued that such emission offsets were permissible under section 110 of the Clean Air Act as long as they did not "interfere with" the attainment or maintenance of the ambient standards (U.S. EPA 1976: 55525).

Three important elements of emission offsets in the agency ruling were: (1) the offset ratio had to be greater than one-for-one (thus, in the agency's view, insuring progress toward attainment); (2) leftover emission offset credit could not be "banked" for future growth;[12] and (3) "external" offsets between sources with separate ownership were permissible. With these key components in the policy, EPA set the policy on a course of air quality improvement rather than mere maintenance, and sidestepped the issue of property rights in air resources temporarily by prohibiting banking.[13] In addition, by tackling the growth ban problem directly in issuing the ruling, EPA sought to generate as much public comment and study as possible to help it address the long-term problem presented by economic growth in "dirty air" areas. Most important for the focus of this study, however, through the offset policy the agency laid the groundwork for establishing at least a limited form of market exchange of emission credits or rights.

According to a number of the EPA staff involved in formulating the offset policy, however, they did not fully realize that they had devised a scheme with the earmarks of an economic incentive device similar to marketable permits. As Liroff argues, "the initial policy was created primarily to solve a political problem, rather than to promote more cost-effective pollution control through creation of a regulated market" (Liroff 1980: 22). It was in further pursuit of the initially prohibited banking concept that EPA staff began to fathom what had been created, and what they had to do to make it work.

As the transition from the Ford to the Carter administration was taking place, a small staff working group in EPA's Office of Planning and Management (the agency's policy arm)[14] was beginning to consider whether offsets, as initially fashioned in the 1976 ruling, would still pose an obstacle to growth and whether the prohibition against banking should be lifted. Staff research indicated, for example, that external or interplant offsets would be hard to generate because of transaction costs created at least in part by restrictions imposed in the agency ruling. The staff working group soon realized that the questions they were pursuing were much larger than merely writing additional agency guidelines. Establishing a system to bank emission offset credits required fundamental institutional changes that would, in effect, create a quasi-market system for the exchange of such credits. In order for such a system to work, a set of legal instruments in the form of interpretations of the Clean Air Act was needed, along with the resolution of significant administrative and technical problems so that an accounting system for the credits could be organized.

The realization by this small group of EPA staff that a program of air pollution offsets with a banking component contained the essence of a quasi-market approach to regulating air pollution that was potentially consistent with the legal requirements of the Clean Air Act, the preferences of Congress notwithstanding (see chapter 3), squared perfectly with the interests of a new administration bent on reform by bringing economic reasoning to decision-making for regulatory programs. As the Carter administration appointees settled into place in the agency, the mission and size of the staff group working on banking was expanded to address the greatly increased level of effort needed to accomplish these broader tasks.

A Rejuvenated Bubble and the Rise of Controlled Trading

The timing of the growth ban crisis in the Clean Air Act, the formulation of an offset remedy, and then the arrival on the scene of the new Carter administration were, therefore, all quite propitious for initiation of full-fledged regulatory reform inside the EPA. In sharp contrast to the circumstances faced by the agency in its early days under President Nixon, environmentalists perceived the Carter administration as the strongest government advocate of environmental protection since the launching of Earth Day. Hence, the Carter administration had somewhat more freedom to act in the environmental policy arena. However, President Carter also came to office with a pledge to bring greater efficiency to the design and operation of government programs, especially regulation (see chapter 1).

Carter's demands for regulatory reform, centered on more extensive regulatory analysis grounded in economic reasoning, reached to the heart of the EPA. Carter's choice for EPA administrator, Douglas Costle, and his assistant administrator for planning and management (OPM), William Drayton, both came from Connecticut state government, which had instituted a program of "economic law enforcement" (the Connecticut Plan) under Costle's direction. Drayton, the Connecticut Enforcement Project's principal architect, explains the underlying concept:[15]

Central to the Connecticut approach is an economic standard that recaptures the gains realized from noncompliance by charging violators an amount just sufficient to make compliance as economically attractive as profitable commercial expenditures, thereby denying scofflaws the unfair advantage they would otherwise have over law-abiding competitors. This recapture standard sets a financial charge exactly fitted to the facts of each case, one that varies directly with the value and duration of noncompliance. (Drayton 1980: 2)

Although the primary concerns of the Connecticut Plan were problems of compliance and enforcement, Drayton clearly intended the design to create an economically rational enforcement mechanism.

The impact of the new administration, with well-defined goals for regulatory program analysis and management, was soon felt in the agency. Drayton greatly invigorated OPM with a resultant change in the balance of power between line and staff offices, particularly between OPM and the program staff responsible for air and water pollution control. Also, because of his close ties to EPA administrator Costle and the Carter White House, Drayton was able to position himself and his staff of analysts to exert much greater influence in EPA's process for making policy decisions. The political fortunes of the agency's small band of economists and other analysts were thus transformed.

The dedication, loyalty, and perseverance in pursuit of the goal of regulatory reform shown by the Carter appointees in the EPA notwithstanding, they could not have accomplished their agenda for expanded use of economic analysis and the search for increased efficiency in regulatory programs within the tightly drawn, command-and-control structure of the Clean Air Act (or in the even more tightly drawn Clean Water Act, for that matter). The political (and statutory) breathing room the Carter people needed came in the form of the grown-ban crisis and its administrative remedy, the offset policy.

Congress incorporated EPA's 1976 offset policy, with modifications, into the 1977 amendments to the Clean Air Act, enacted in August of that year. Application of the policy was limited to the period up to July 1, 1979, the deadline for states to have new state implementation plans approved by EPA. Congress also included an alternative approach to addressing growth in nonattainment areas. The lawmakers provided that prior to July 1, 1979 states could waive the requirement for offsets if they required existing sources to control emissions beyond what would merely be required for attainment of the ambient standards. States following this course would be creating a margin for growth that would allow new sources to enter an area. After July 1, 1979, Congress anticipated, an offset approach *or* a growth margin approach would be adopted by each state that would govern new economic development in nonattainment areas under a state's revised SIP.

Despite its origins as a political solution to a major policy dilemma, therefore, the offset policy proved to be just the tool the EPA reformers needed to put a chink in the command-and-control armor of the Clean Air Act and begin an effort toward reform of air pollution regulation using economic incentives, a reform effort which would be fully consistent with the Carter agenda for better regulatory management based on expanded economic analysis and increased efficiency in regulatory programs. Under the direction of Drayton, the agency pursued a three-pronged approach to reform, including a revised offset policy, resurrection of the bubble, and consolidation of staff resources.

The Offset Policy Revised. The revised offset ruling EPA issued in January 1979 imposed a series of conditions, revised slightly from the 1976 rules (see U.S. EPA 1979a: 3284) that included lowest achievable emissions rate (LAER) requirements at proposed new sources (as specified in the 1976 offset ruling and endorsed by Congress in the 1977 amendments to the Clean Air Act) and demonstrations of net air quality benefit from offset arrangements. Furthermore, the revised ruling prohibited netting (or bubbles) where the offset ruling applied and where bans on construction were in effect. Yet the new rules granted states permission to allow netting (or bubbles) if approved state implementation plans were in effect (see Levin 1982: 70; Liroff 1986: 126).

Most important for the drive toward incentive-based reform, the 1979 offset ruling reversed the 1976 rules and allowed states to bank "excess" emission reductions. The reformers in the agency accomplished this policy reversal by finding in the 1977 Clean Air Act amendments the solution to the internal agency debate over whether surplus emission reductions were conceivable in nonattainment areas. EPA contended in its 1976 ruling: "To allow . . . 'banking' would be inconsistent with a basic policy of the Act and the ruling—namely, that at a minimum, no new source should be allowed to make existing NAAQS violations any worse" (U.S. EPA 1976: 55526). The agency explained in its 1979 ruling, however:

The Clean Air Act Amendments of 1977 modified [the restriction on banking] by allowing States to incorporate provisions for growth in SIP plans for nonattainment areas. Under Section 173(1) of the Act, emission reductions are compared to a "reasonable further progress" goal, and reductions beyond the minimum requirement may be used to offset future growth. In essence, the State becomes the banker and must decide how to allocate the banked emissions. (U.S. EPA 1979a: 3280)

Hence the agency (and, at least in EPA's interpretation, Congress as well) found that the alternative "growth allowance" solution to the growth ban in the Clean Air Act allowed banking (and also from the agency reformers' perspective, established the possibility for a regulated market in pollution) because ". . . surplus emission reductions . . . might legitimately be created in nonattainment areas so long as they did not *interfere* with progress toward attainment" (Levin 1982: 70, emphasis in original). This was of course the rationale the agency used to justify emission offsets in 1976 when it also rejected banking of those offsets. Some EPA staff and outside observers, however, insisted that growth margins or growth allowances created by the states did not signify surplus emission reductions. The additional assimilative capacity of the air in a region created by tightening control requirements under a growth allowance strategy, they argued, would be used up by economic expansion and the construction of new industrial facilities creating pollution. Perhaps, then, some decision makers in the agency had bigger objectives in mind by reversing the decision on banking, as the comments by Michael Levin suggest. "This banking provision was particularly crucial. It laid the basis for readily available reductions that could . . . encourage firms to meet emission requirements through trades. It also enlarged opportunities for . . . savings, since cost-effective combinations of emission increases and decreases seldom occur at the same time" (Levin 1982: 70).

Although the bubble for existing sources became the core of the coordinated regulatory reform effort led by Carter appointees and their hand-picked career staff in the agency, the offset and growth allowance provisions in the Clean Air Act and EPA's interpretation of them clearly paved the way for all the EPA reforms to carry the imprimatur of an economic incentives rationale; and, of course, such a rationale was quite consistent with the broader Carter administration policy agenda of using economic analysis to increase the efficiency of regulatory programs. Offsets became the crucial means toward this aim once EPA staff recognized the potential for creating a quasi-market system that was manifest in a system of air pollution offsets with a banking component. As the head of the EPA staff group working on banking contended during an interview (a view of banking which some of his colleagues denied existed):

What we [created was] the equivalent of such a system. We just created a set of legal instruments that looked different. It was grafted onto the existing regulatory system. . . . [E]xcept for a few technology-forcing requirements, [offsets] constitute the equivalent of a system of marketable permits. We just don't call it that. But there is really no difference in terms of the way it functions, the administrative procedures you have to use, or its economic outcomes.

More than just a reform, of course, the offset ruling was a political necessity. No one in the EPA with an agency point of view, even if he did not accept the use of economic incentives to reform environmental regulation as part of the agency's governing ethos, was willing to mount a direct challenge to the offset concept and the statutory interpretation on which EPA justified banking.[16] Thus the door was opened through which incentive-based regulatory reform, and in parallel the push to alter the organizational character of the agency needed to make the reform movement successful, entered and took hold in the agency.

The Bubble Returns. The rejuvenation of the bubble began in 1977 on a track independent from the work on offsets and banking. One of the first areas of economic policy to receive attention in the Carter administration was the sorry plight of the domestic steel industry. American steel manufacturers were in dire straits, suffering from the triple blows of low-priced foreign competition, aging and outmoded plants and equipment, and poor management. In addition, steel had a record as one of the most recalcitrant industries in the fight for clean air. During 1975 hearings on reauthorization of the Clean Air Act, the following exchange between Rep. Paul Rogers (D-FL) and executives of major steel companies took place (cited in U.S. House 1977: 210–211).

Mr. Rogers. Let's see, we have had the law 5 years now. Could you tell me, company by company, how many of your plants are in compliance presently and how many are not?

Mr. Armour [Interlake, Inc.]. I think we have to define in compliance with what.

Mr. Rogers. The Clean Air Act?

Mr. Amour. We do not have any in compliance.

Mr. Anderson [Bethlehem Steel Corp.]. None.

Mr. Jaicks [Inland Steel Co.]. None.

Mr. Mallick [U.S. Steel Co.]. None.

Mr. Tucker [National Steel Corp.]. We have no plants in compliance.

Given the steel industry's compliance record, it is not surprising that EPA made steel, along with smelters and utilities, the focus of a special enforcement effort in 1977. However, the cries of the steel industry for government attention to its predicament, including claims that environmental regulations were an important source of the industry's problems, were heeded by the Carter administration. Undersecretary of the Treasury Anthony Solomon chaired a special interagency task force to review federal policies that might be contributing to the decline in the domestic steel industry. The steel companies mostly sought tax relief and trade protection, but they also urged the Solomon committee to recommend that EPA consider using a bubble concept devised by ARMCO, Inc., for its Middletown, Ohio plant.

The Solomon committee issued its report in December 1977 without any specific recommendations about environmental regulations, but as part of the administration-wide effort to respond to the report, EPA held a series of meetings with steel industry executives. While making no promises to the steel executives, internally and to the White House the agency committed itself to evaluating the possibilities of the bubble. Initially, the burden for evaluating the bubble fell on the Office of Air, Noise, and Radiation, headed by Assistant Administrator David Hawkins. Hawkins, however, was not enthusiastic about the idea, nor was his staff prepared for the added workload, preoccupied as it was with administering the basic air pollution control programs, along with a series of court-ordered compliance schedules for major steel producers won through numerous civil suits against the steel industry. EPA Administrator Costle decided then to transfer responsibility for evaluating the bubble to William Drayton's Office of Planning and Management.

In the spring of 1978, OPM headed an agency-wide task force to examine the legal and technical feasibility of bubbles for both air and water pollution.[17] The task force chose four principal criteria for evaluating the bubble concept: legality, enforceability, environmental acceptability, and economic efficiency (see U.S. EPA 1978). The greater efficiency of the bubble was a foregone conclusion, given the motivations, interests, and perspective of the EPA officials who chose the bubble as the centerpiece of their reform efforts. Moreover, staff in the Air Programs and Enforcement offices, with their specialized concerns for legality, enforceability, and environmental impact, were hardly prepared to challenge the bubble on economic efficiency grounds. Legal obstacles were quickly removed by interpretations of the Clean Air Act supplied by EPA's general counsel, despite some objections from her staff. General Counsel Joan Z. (Jodie) Bernstein early on took a liking to incentive-based reform ideas and signed on as a strong ally of OPM's Drayton. The remaining issues of enforceability and environmental acceptability therefore became the focus of the debate within the agency over the wisdom of resurrecting the bubble concept, especially with the specter of the steel industry's recalcitrance looming over the agency. "The impact of the bubble on sources' existing obligations to abate pollution was an especially important concern . . . , many areas had failed to attain standards [and] sources' noncompliance with obligations was a major contributor to nonattainment" (Liroff 1986: 39).

Although attempting to tread the middle ground between the desires of EPA's reformers to push the bubble ahead as part of the larger incentive-based reform effort, and the fears about enforceability and environmental acceptability expressed by the Air Programs and Enforcement offices, the task force's September 1978 report largely reflected the views of Assistant Administrator Hawkins and his staff. The worries of Hawkins and his staff, and what to do about them while still making a stab at getting the bubble concept to work, continued to dominate the early shaping of a rejuvenated bubble concept when EPA published its bubble proposal in January 1979. In presenting its proposal, the agency argued that its "alternative emissions reduction option" would "promote greater economic efficiency and increased technological innovation" (U.S. EPA 1979b: 3741).

Yet the proposal contained a series of conditions tacked on to the basic concept, conditions which reflected Hawkins's objectives in agreeing to allow the bubble for existing air pollution sources to go forward: (1) all air quality standards had to be met, that is, bubbles would only be allowed in areas with approved SIPs projecting attainment by statutory deadlines; (2) pollutants traded under any proposed bubble would have to be comparable; (3) proposed bubbles could not replace existing SIP provisions; (4) each emission point included in a bubble would have to have a specific emissions limit tied to enforceable testing techniques; (5) no noncomplying source could submit a bubble proposal; (6) existing compliance dates could not be extended; and (7) no delays in existing enforcement actions would be allowed.

Although opponents of the bubble and regulatory reform generally had essentially won the early rounds in the internal agency battle, to EPA's reformers the substantive content of the bubble proposal, with its severe restrictions, was less important than the agency's public commitment to reform.

> More important than . . . content, however, was the fact that the agency had made the proposal public and committed itself to further publicity. For the first time, a rudimentary implementation strategy would accompany a proposed systemwide reform in environmental regulation. (Levin 1982: 75)

Moreover, the reformers were succeeding in transforming the relevant terms of agency policy deliberations. A policy proposal with phrases such as "greater economic efficiency" and "increased technological innovation" indicated that cost considerations and efficiency, as criteria for evaluating alternative regulatory options, and seen as anathema to the proper concerns of environmental policy by adherents to the agency's original enforcement culture, were no longer being ignored. The agency had begun to accept the language, if not yet all the ideas, embodied in a culture of efficiency.

The agency's bubble proposal elicited a large volume of comments covering a wide range of positive and negative arguments. Environmentalists contended that the bubble was not environmentally acceptable and that the steel industry had promoted it as the means to escape legal requirements. Environmentalists also wondered whether EPA wanted to be aligned, through endorsement of the bubble concept, with an industry having such a poor compliance record. Numerous state pollution control agencies argued that the bubble was unnecessary because states could already adopt such an approach under existing SIP provisions. The states also argued that EPA's independent promotion of the bubble would add administrative and resource burdens to state activity that state agencies would find difficult to handle. Support for the bubble, and for lifting of many of the restrictions included in EPA's proposal, came from a host of industries in addition to steel, and from a number of other federal agencies.

The arguments of outside commentators regarding the agency's proposal proved to be of insufficient weight on either side of the debate to resolve the internal agency dispute over the final shape of the concept. The comment process did serve the agency's reformers well, however, by identifying for them those individuals and organizations that could be counted on as an external constituency for the bubble. The building of such an external constituency by the OPM staff served to further legitimize, and boost the political support for, regulatory reform in the EPA (see Levin 1982: 76).

EPA published the final bubble rule in December 1979 (U.S. EPA 1979c). The final rule lifted a number of the restrictions contained in the January proposal but retained others. Unlike the proposed rules, the final rule granted permission for bubbles over multiple plants, for extensions of compliance deadlines in some circumstances, and for trades involving open dust sources. Like the January proposal, however, each bubble would still be treated as an individual SIP revision, thus retaining perhaps the ultimate safeguard sought by critics of the concept within the agency: each bubble proposal would be subject to federal approval, giving program staff at EPA headquarters the chance to review individual bubble applications (although the bubble program would be the responsibility of OPM).

The liberalization of the bubble in the final December ruling was only a small step forward, in concrete program and organizational terms, for the kind of change sought by EPA's regulatory reformers. Organizational changes and the reallocation of staff resources accompanying the establishment of an official EPA bubble policy were limited (see the expanded discussion in the next section; also see Levin 1982: 77). But the situation changed quickly as two events associated with the requirement in the December 1979 final rule that bubbles be approved as individual SIP revisions gave major impetus to expansion of the bubble, and this in turn accelerated regulatory reform in the agency.

First, in early 1980 New Jersey proposed to revise its SIP to include a "generic" bubble regulation to allow existing sources of volatile organic compounds to use bubbles to achieve compliance. The state proposed to review a bubble proposal submitted by a source, but would not submit the bubble to EPA as a SIP revision. Second, at a national conference on regulatory reform convened by EPA in September 1980, the message senior EPA officials received both from the states and industry representatives was that the SIP revision requirement was a major stumbling block in getting bubbles approved that would save industry millions of dollars in control costs.

Together, these two events signaled an important new stage in the evolution of regulatory reform in the EPA because they were linked to a further shift in the balance of power to the reform side. Opposition to incentive-based reform remained vigorous within the agency even after EPA approved New Jersey's generic bubble conditionally in November 1980 (U.S. EPA 1980b) and gave final approval in April 1981 (U.S. EPA 1981b), but the efforts of the reformers to "sell" regulatory reform in the hinterlands had finally borne fruit, sparking a movement for reform outside the agency that could not be denied inside. In addition, reform acquired further organizational legitimacy when the previously empty concept of "controlled trading" of emissions gained real substance as the umbrella concept for the agency's multiple incentive-based reform efforts through consolidation under the aegis of the newly created Regulatory Reform Staff (see the discussion in the next section). Sadly for the Carter administration reformers in the EPA, however, these final events of 1980 together formed the penultimate chapter in their search for comprehensive, economically rational reform of environmental regulation.

Through the remainder of 1980 and the early days of 1981, the agency continued to take additional incremental steps toward further liberalization of the bubble and the consolidation of the air pollution regulatory reform effort. As the last act of the Carter reformers, EPA Administrator Costle issued a press release, just a few days before Ronald Reagan's inauguration, announcing several changes to streamline administrative review of bubbles and to make them more readily available. A "controlled trading" Federal Register notice was planned to give final, formal recognition to reform of air pollution regulation as fundamental agency policy, but the political leadership in the EPA ran out of time as their president's tenure in office drew to a close.

Organizing and Staffing Regulatory Reform. Clearly, for regulatory reform as a coordinated effort to survive the transition to a new presidential administration, EPA career staff would have to carry the torch. Through a series of minor but important organizational changes and reallocations of resources, the Carter reformers laid the groundwork to insure that career policy staff would continue to labor at incentive-based reform. Beginning in 1977, William Drayton, EPA's assistant administrator for planning and management, made organization and staffing decisions that served to institutionalize his regulatory reform objectives, first in his own policy division, and eventually throughout the organization.

As this chronicle has already noted, Drayton and his policy staff recognized the crucial importance of offsets and banking in any scheme to bring incentive-based reform to air pollution regulation. As soon as possible after becoming acclimated to the agency, the reformers in EPA's policy office increased the size of the staff working on emission offsets and expanded the scope of its work in the search for a statutorily acceptable lever for regulatory reform. It was from this OPM staff group and its concern with making banking of emission offsets for future use a reality that controlled trading as a comprehensive concept covering netting, bubbles, and offsets would arise.

As has also been noted, OPM was the lead office for the work of the bubble concept task force because EPA Administrator Costle had transferred responsibility for studying the bubble option from David Hawkins, who was in charge of EPA's air programs, to Drayton, who was keenly interested in making the bubble the centerpiece of his efforts at reforming EPA regulations. Denoting its importance to any reform effort, Drayton gave responsibility for this work on the bubble to OPM's economic analysis division. The results of the work of the bubble concept task force, and OPM's central role in that work, led to the most significant organizational and resource changes associated with the movement for regulatory reform in the EPA. First, in late 1979 a separate staff, albeit small and supported with only $50,000 in emergency funds (Levin 1982: 77), was set up within OPM's economic analysis division to implement the newly finalized bubble policy. Second, as part of the final bubble rule, EPA designated bubble coordinators in the air programs staff of each region to respond to state agency and industry inquiries about the bubble and aid in developing bubble applications (U.S. EPA 1979c: 71780, 71788). Thus the reform effort was not only affecting the organization and staffing of the policy office, but was beginning to affect the operations of program offices as well.

Third, and most important to the institutionalization of reform in EPA, Drayton created in late 1979 a separate entity to pursue his most important objective. Dubbed the Regulatory Reform Staff (RRS), Drayton placed this new OPM entity under the ostensible control of the economic analysis division, but gave it considerable autonomy. Drayton placed the RRS in the hands of Michael Levin, previously with the White House staff and the Occupational Safety and Health Administration in the Labor Department, who was dedicated to the transformation of how the agency went about its regulatory business. Over the ensuing months, Levin assembled a staff of analysts, researchers, and individuals interested in marketing new ideas from within OPM, from EPA program offices, and from the staffs of EPA consultants and contractors doing business with the policy office.

Drayton initially charged the Regulatory Reform Staff only with coordinating the work of other OPM staff groups involved in implementing netting, bubbles, offsets, and banking. Levin, who continues to serve as chief of the Regulatory Reform Staff, quickly realized that coordination was a dubious undertaking. "It soon became apparent that 'coordination' would not work where these projects were in separate divisions, were not answerable to the coordinating office, and were composed of close-knit staffs who viewed coordination as interference. The clear answer was a reorganization to bring these projects under common control" (Levin 1982: 78).

An interim answer to the problem of coordination before reorganization could be achieved was to create a common language emphasizing the similarities and interconnections among the disparate reform programs. Thus arose the idea of controlled trading from the work on offsets and banking, in which, as one EPA staff person put it, "a credit was a credit was a credit," whether it was generated initially in association with a bubble, an offset, or netting. As Levin further explains the idea:

The vague concept of "controlled trading" was duly given content to describe how all these reforms made extra control profitable by letting firms trade inexpensive reductions created at one point and time for expensive regulatory requirements on other points at different times, under controlled conditions to assure air quality and enforceability. (Levin 1982: 78)

An umbrella concept for the multiple policy changes the policy office was advocating, which would fold into the notion of a comprehensive approach to reform, was not without its detractors within RRS. As one former member of the Regulatory Reform staff described the situation in mid–1983:

There were two camps here. I can't say I was the leader of one camp, but I was in one camp that said, "Go ahead with the incremental changes." Another camp said, "No, let's wait and we'll tie banking, netting, and the bubble policy all together in the emissions trading policy statement." Okay, we decided to put it all together, put all our eggs in one basket and watch that basket. Well, consequently, it's been two years and we haven't come out with a final policy statement. . . . Had we come out with these [incremental] changes, we'd have had another one-and-one-half years' experience. We could have come out then with a *Federal Register* notice saying, "This register notice ties together the previous 10 notices," and now we've got the policy. Instead, we are . . . still at the proposed policy [stage] and two notices to go.

Nevertheless, reform packaged comprehensively did prevail, and it is arguably the case that the comprehensive approach was necessary for the success of the top-down programmatic *and organizational* reform sought by William Drayton. Hence, perhaps the most important observation one can make about the organization and staff changes that were part and parcel of the regulatory reform movement in the agency is that although offsets and banking were the statutory keys to unlocking the potential for incentive-based reform of EPA's air pollution regulatory programs, reorganization, reallocation of staff resources, and, possibly most important, *marketing reform with a single sales pitch*, provided the power to open the unlocked door and unleash reform within the agency.

With the establishment of the RRS, regulatory reform in the EPA was soon on a fast track. January 1980 saw the administrator's budget guidance for fiscal year 1981 include controlled trading as a top regional priority (Levin 1982: 78–79). In June 1980 the first bubble applications began arriving at EPA headquarters and the entire bubble project was transferred to the Regulatory Reform Staff. In September the RRS held its regulatory reform conference. Major increases in staff and budget for the bubble, and the reorganization of offsets and banking into RRS followed the conference. In November, EPA conditionally approved New Jersey's generic bubble regulation, and in January 1981, outgoing EPA Administrator Costle made his announcement easing further some restrictions on the bubble.

From Controlled Trading to Emissions Trading

The momentum for regulatory reform in the agency was at its peak when all activity came to a lurching halt with the inauguration of President Reagan. The broadly encompassing "controlled trading" policy statement, subsuming netting, bubbles, offsets, and banking, was waiting in the wings to be unveiled in the *Federal Register*. Nevertheless, it would have to wait until an entirely new set of actors took their positions on stage. The change in administrations brought a new chapter to the evolution of regulatory reform in the EPA, and one that can serve to conclude this emissions trading chronicle.

True to the efforts of William Drayton to institutionalize regulatory reform in the EPA, the RRS headed by Levin was determined to succeed in bringing comprehensive, incentive-based reform to the agency's major air pollution control programs. The task proved especially difficult, however. The work of RRS to get the controlled trading policy statement it had drafted accepted by the agency as official policy met with continued resistance from staff in the agency's air programs, suffered from the chaos of transition, including unfilled and temporary appointments to key political positions in the agency, and encountered additional resistance from President Reagan's choice for EPA administrator, Anne Gorsuch Burford.

Again, chapters 5 and 6 explore more fully the nature of some of the key objections expressed by EPA's Air Programs and Enforcement offices, the locus of internal agency opposition to emissions trading. It is especially noteworthy, however, that the RRS found itself in a difficult position even before the Reagan appointees set up shop because Walter Barber, a career civil servant who served as head of the Office of Air Quality Planning and Standards under David Hawkins in the Carter administration EPA, was acting administrator during the transition. According to other EPA staff, while not expressing blanket opposition to incentive-based reform or the concept of controlled trading, Barber was critically concerned with the implementation approach being taken by the Regulatory Reform Staff. As one EPA official who served in the administrator's office for both Costle and Burford explained:

[Barber] was concerned, I believe, with procedure in terms of the implementation of the policy. He was concerned procedurally largely because of the ambiguity of what [RRS] was pushing at the time. [RRS] had basically 20 pages of concept and was pushing that as a *Federal Register* notice. I think that Barber's clear and correct presumption was that if we were that ambiguous, we would end up in a worse situation than we are now because we'd end up with years of litigation.

Barber's concerns clearly put a brake on the momentum RRS had built up for controlled trading going into the transition, and with that momentum slowed, the arrival of appointees from the new administration brought the development of emissions trading and incentive-based regulatory reform to a dead stop. The transition from a moderate-to-liberal Democratic administration to perhaps the most conservative Republican administration in half a century brought enormous instability to an organization with liberal social movement roots like the EPA. Exacerbating this instability was the continuing flux and turnover in key political positions in the agency, including the Office of General Counsel and the Office of Planning and Management. The EPA had three general counsels in its first two years. The first assistant administrator for planning and management resigned after six months, the second nominee withdrew under a cloud of suspicion about outside business dealings, and the third had to serve for six months in an acting capacity.

Beyond the leadership flux and the accompanying lack of policy guidance, the Reagan appointees presented the Regulatory Reform Staff with a massive education and selling problem. Although regulatory reforms like controlled trading appeared to fit neatly into the Reagan agenda on regulation, EPA career staff soon recognized that subtle but clear distinctions existed between the Carter notion of regulatory reform and the Reagan notion of regulatory relief (see the related discussion in chapter 1). Thus what the RRS was pushing quickly became stigmatized as "a warmed-over Carter administration idea," to quote one staff person from the General Counsel's Office, or worse, ". . . a Democratic smoke screen to divert attention from the 'real issues' of federal intrusion and overly stringent regulation" (Levin 1982: 88). The Reagan camp was also concerned that reforming air pollution regulation along the lines of controlled trading would actually serve to undermine the President's objectives for radically revising the Clean Air Act.

Chipping away at this mountain of resistance took the Regulatory Reform Staff more than a year, especially because their energies were spread over two more fronts in addition to the campaign to educate and win over the agency's new political leadership. The RRS was locked in continued negotiations with agency opponents and skeptics over the exact language that would be included in any controlled trading policy statement, and the RRS had to work constantly at keeping a high profile for the reforms in the regions, in the states, and in industry. To overcome these obstacles to its version of reform, the RRS employed a dual strategy: (1) brute bureaucratic force with paper (or "briefing documents") as the principal weapon; and (2) the help of the outside constituency for regulatory reform assembled by RRS, including industry leaders and members of the Carter and Reagan administrations, especially members of the Council of Economic Advisors and the White House Domestic Policy Staff. As a dramatic example, here is how one member of the Regulatory Reform Staff described the process of convincing Administrator Burford of the merits of controlled trading:

Anne had come in [after having] made her famous speech to the American Enterprise Institute, which blasted the use of economic incentives. She was basically a trial lawyer. She thought [incentives] had lots of political downsides and not much political benefit. She didn't understand how the programs operated. She didn't understand how the bureaucracy operated. It turned out that that was a very easy problem to solve from our perspective because the thing that solved it was a campaign we had very little to do with in which a whole bunch of different senior industry people contacted her essentially in defense of the bubble policy. They said, "We have this pending policy and it needs to be liberalized. We can use it in many more circumstances. It would save billions of dollars for the economy. You're crazy not to support it." There was also a lot of pressure from the White House.

Incrementally, RRS began to generate new momentum. In March 1981 the agency proposed to allow netting for new source review in nonattainment areas (see U.S. EPA 1981a, and the final rule published in U.S. EPA 1981c). In May the agency's Steering Committee approved a draft controlled trading policy statement (Levin 1982: 84). Nonetheless Administrator Burford objected both to the title of the document and to what she considered its inordinate length and incomprehensibility. Burford spent a week editing the document with the help of her staff, and sent it back to RRS for further work. The results of Burford's personal intervention in the process were twofold: (1) "controlled trading," which to Burford and others smacked too much of regulatory intrusiveness, became "emissions trading," a relatively neutral term; and (2) the large document was split in two, with a short, distilled "emissions trading policy statement" accompanied by a "technical issues document."

By the fall of 1981 Burford was prepared to announce the new EPA policy in a speech, but RRS was not prepared to deliver a final document that had cleared all the hurdles of internal agency processing, known as "red boarder" review. Finally, after additional haggling, negotiations, and tension between RRS and the administrator's office, reform of air pollution regulation in comprehensive form saw the light of day in April 1982 with Burford's announcement of the proposed Emissions Trading Policy Statement (ETPS) and its simultaneous publication in the *Federal Register* (U.S. EPA 1982).

The battle was not over by any measure. Additional conflict within the agency surrounding the issues of plant shutdowns (see chapter 6) and bubbles in nonattainment areas without EPA-approved attainment projections remained to be resolved. The agency also would go through more political turmoil and two more changes in top leadership before a final policy statement on emissions trading could be issued (for more detail on continued development of emissions trading after 1982, see Liroff 1986: 55–60, 130–131, 147–148). Nevertheless, the EPA's regulatory reformers achieved a major milestone with the publication of the proposed policy.

CONCLUSION

In presenting this chronicle of the rise of emissions trading, I have attempted to highlight both the programmatic and the political and organizational dimensions of the achievements realized by regulatory reformers in the EPA. As the chronicle fully illustrates, in programmatic terms the EPA reformers developed and implemented important new agency policy that political appointees and career personnel alike could scarcely have conceived of 10 years earlier. More profound, however, were the political and organizational changes wrought by the reformers. But the chronicle gives only a taste of the political controversies generated by the attempt to incorporate economic incentive ideas into the agency's air pollution control programs. Much more also needs to be said about the changes in the organizational dynamics of the agency associated with the movement for regulatory reform.

Two important tasks therefore remain for this study of bureaucratic politics and regulatory reform in the EPA. The first task is to look more closely at the political issues raised by the development of emissions trading and the larger drive for regulatory reform in the agency. The second task is to consider more fully the nature of the organizational changes in the EPA linked to the development of emissions trading, and what these changes might reveal about organizational leadership, policy making in administrative agencies, and related questions of politics and reform in public organizations. The remaining chapters take up these tasks.

NOTES

1. James Cameron provides a useful definition of ideology that encompasses both political beliefs and professional value systems. "Ideology refers to a shared system of beliefs and values that provides reasons for action with accompanying rules of logic. It emerges out of the social situation and provides a framework for viewing it. *This holds for the generation of a scientific or professional belief system as well as a political doctrine"* (Cameron 1978: 541, emphasis added).

2. The description provided here is based on EPA's proposed "Emissions Trading Policy Statement" (U.S. EPA 1982). Although technically only a proposal, EPA published the proposal as interim guidelines, which took effect immediately. This meant that EPA would operate as if emissions trading was fully operational agency policy. Continuing controversy within the agency over various elements of the program delayed the issuance of a final version of the policy statement for over four years. The policy was finalized in December 1986 (see U.S. EPA 1986). See Liroff (1986) for an account of the post–1982 controversies and their resolution.

3. After the publication of the ETPS in 1982, EPA tried to expand the bubble concept to new sources of pollution (see U.S. EPA 1985, for more detail). Analysis of the impact of this program expansion is outside the scope of the present study, however.

4. This has proved to be one of the most controversial issues in the genesis of emissions trading, reflecting the tug-of-war between adherents to the agency's original culture of enforcement and champions of a greater emphasis on economic analysis and efficiency. As part of the examination of the ideological conflicts generated by regulatory reform in the EPA, chapter 6 explores some of the particulars in the debate over safeguards.

5. Some passages in the lengthy account that follows are based solely on the recollections of current and former EPA personnel and outside observers. Such recollections were, as much as possible, corroborated in other interviews, but little independent documentary evidence was available to verify them further.

6. It is important to note that in both its proposed and final rules on this subject, EPA never identified the source of the pressure for the changes, citing only the comments of "interested parties," including "industry" and "state and federal agencies" (see U.S. EPA 1975). It is the record of the court case (ASARCO, Inc. v. EPA) triggered by these changes in EPA's regulations that reveals the exact source and nature of the political pressure brought to bear on the agency.

7. A number of EPA staff people interviewed for this study argued that the bubble concept devised by the agency was "nothing new" and that a number of states had experimented with such optional emission reduction devices under the discretion to consider alternative pollution control strategies granted to the states by the SIP provision (section 110) of the Clean Air Act. This claim was reiterated by Harry Williams, head of the State and Territorial Air Pollution Program Administrators, in testimony on a later iteration of the bubble (see Liroff 1986: 44). Levin (1982: 75) challenges the claim. This early state activity and any lessons learned from it seem to have played no role in the design of the bubble at EPA headquarters, however, or in the central importance assumed by the bubble concept in EPA's subsequent drive for regulatory reform.

8. To a considerable extent, variations in the nomenclature of the program components of emissions trading stem more from what kinds of sources are involved (that is, new versus existing, in attainment or nonattainment areas) than in the kind of trading arrangements contemplated. Hence, an emissions trade within a single plant may be an internal offset if it involves major modification of a source, or a bubble if it involves an existing source trying to meet control requirements more efficiently. There are technical differences between these two types of trades, but they go beyond the level of detail necessary for purposes of this study.

9. Compliance bubbles are similar to applicability bubbles in that the former are also created by changes in regulations, especially the definition of "affected facilities" for selected industries covered by NSPS.

10. Some may object to my characterization of these policy changes as "circumscribed" because they were the result, and cause, of major administrative, legislative, and judicial action involving the PSD program, culminating in the December 1979 decision by the D.C. Circuit Court in Alabama Power Co. v. Costle (636 F.2d 323). That decision upheld and expanded EPA's regulations for netting in PSD areas. From the perspective of this study, however, those policy actions were secondary because they were not the central stimulus for the regulatory reform movement in the agency, but rather were swept along as the drive for reform gained momentum. See Liroff (1986: 117–124) for a full account.

11. A draft of EPA's offset policy had been circulated to state agencies for com-

ment in the spring of 1976. EPA staff and outside observers disagree in retrospect about the extent to which the activity involving SOHIO in California, and the informal offset policy employed by EPA's Region IX office (San Francisco), shaped the offset ruling. Overall, the west coast activity appears to have played little role in the internal politics of the development of the offset policy at EPA headquarters.

12. The entire concept of banking emission offsets hinged on acceptance of the principle that excess credit or surplus reductions could in fact be generated in nonattainment areas. As the argument of one side in the agency debate held, any additional emission reductions achieved were not surplus because they should contribute to bringing an area into attainment. See the more extensive discussion of this issue in chapter 6.

13. The property rights issue reemerged in connection with questions about banking and surplus emission reductions and with questions about so-called "shutdown" credits in the emissions trading program. See chapter 6 for further discussion.

14. This office has gone through a number of name changes, including the Office of Policy and Resource Management, and currently, the Office of Policy, Planning and Evaluation. Nonetheless, its mission has remained virtually unchanged since its inception as the Office of Planning and Evaluation: to evaluate EPA programs, analyze alternative regulatory approaches, and recommend appropriate options.

15. Drayton also served for a time as the chair of the Regulatory Council. As the EPA's principal advocate for the use of economic incentives in regulation, Drayton sharply disagreed with CEA Chairman Charles Schultze over the specific form economic incentives should take in regulatory programs. Schultze was a staunch advocate of charges. Drayton saw charges as impractical, hence his idea of economic law enforcement (Drayton was a lawyer by training) and his interest in the bubble concept and controlled trading.

16. According to an EPA Region V official, opposition to banking did arise in the Region V office, and the office financed a small study of possible legal challenges to emissions credit banking. (Copy of untitled, undated report available in author's files.)

17. Although the task force included recommendations for use of the bubble in water pollution control in its final report, and EPA staff worked on regulatory changes to implement a water bubble, the short-term prospects for such action were very poor. As a number of EPA officials related in interviews, Thomas Jorling, the assistant administrator in charge of EPA's water programs, who had served as an aide to Edmund Muskie in the Senate, was unalterably opposed to the bubble concept. He enlisted the help of his former boss in fighting the idea of the bubble for water pollution control. The impact of Jorling's fight against the bubble, with the weight of Edmund Muskie's political influence behind it, was devastating to regulatory reform in water pollution control. EPA is only now beginning to make substantial headway on water pollution control reforms (see U.S. EPA 1985: 12–15).

5

CHALLENGES TO IMPLEMENTATION

In this chapter and the next, I endeavor to look closely at just a few of the many controversial issues spawned by the movement for incentive-based regulatory reform in the EPA and the implementation of the movement's principal programmatic effort: emissions trading. A careful assessment of these complex issues and the character of the political divisions associated with them, both within the EPA and among interested parties outside the agency, reinforces the link between regulatory reform and the professional character and governing ethos of the agency.

This chapter concentrates on challenges to implementation. It begins with a brief accounting of some of the numerous debates engendered by the development of emissions trading, as identified by individuals interviewed for this study or cited in other published research on the program. The chapter then moves to a more detailed consideration of three critical issues associated with the implementation of emissions trading, arguing that these disputes over program implementation can be traced to basic questions raised about practicability. This exploration of implementation issues at a relatively high level of generality lays the groundwork for a much more intense examination of the philosophical and ideological conflicts underlying the disputes about legality, technique, and administrative practice generated by emissions trading.

EMISSIONS TRADING AND THE PROBLEMS OF IMPLEMENTATION

The greatest share of controversial issues surrounding the development of emissions trading has concerned the legal and technical difficulties EPA reformers have faced in putting the idea of an incentive-based approach to air pollution control into practice. The program's implementation problems have been exacerbated, of course, by the intricacies and flaws of the existing administrative framework for air pollution control and its underlying statutory foundation.

Considerable debate occurred in the agency, for example, over how much independence from EPA scrutiny the Clean Air Act granted states in developing, revising, and carrying out state implementation plans (SIPs) for achieving the national ambient standards. A narrow interpretation of the flexibility the Clean Air Act grants states regarding SIPs would pose a significant obstacle to implementing emissions trading because extensive federal regulatory oversight and intervention would act to stunt the program's potential, relying as heavily as it does on decentralized decision making. EPA reformers thus sought a broad interpretation of state discretion under the act (Liroff 1986: 12).

Disputes over the interpretation of other portions of the Clean Air Act have also thrown legal obstacles in the way of EPA's reformers. Because Congress left the meaning of many important terms in the act ambiguous, agency policy makers, as well as the courts, have spent considerable time and energy debating the definition of key terms like "source," "plant," and "facility." The redefinitions fashioned by EPA reformers were critical to the evolution of emissions trading. Debate over these redefinitions and subsequent litigation have inhibited more rapid, orderly progress in the implementation of the program (for more detail on emissions trading legal issues, see Liroff 1986: 123–128; also see chapter 4).

Skepticism about the credibility and reliability of state plans, including those already given EPA approval, also sparked debate over the implementation of emissions trading within the agency. The SIPs depend on inventories of emissions in a region developed by counting emissions from existing sources and estimating future emissions from models of economic growth and industrial activity. These models trace where new emissions may originate and where existing emission sources may disappear. Furthermore, the SIPs themselves are based on assumptions about the relationship between emissions and air quality, and the nature of the threats particular pollutants pose to human health. The rush to establish SIPs, spurred by tight initial deadlines in the Clean Air Act, and the embryonic nature of the science of understanding and predicting air quality and its impact on human health, have led many to question seriously assumptions underlying state plans and doubt the quality of emission inventories (Liroff 1986: 12–13).

Many individuals who were party to the development of emissions trading shared the view expressed by Michael Levin, chief of EPA's Regulatory Reform Staff, who contended that there were (and still are) "gross defects in air quality management," including "large gaps in inventories of actual emissions; huge inefficiencies of politically expedient engineering requirements that treated similar industrial processes identically; poorly understood relations between emissions and air quality; [and] inadequate SIPs that EPA was compelled to approve in order to avoid writing local plans itself" (Levin 1982: 65).

A poor air quality accounting system would appear to pose a significant obstacle to successfully implementing emissions trading. "Only by accounting for all emissions in an accurate emissions inventory and relating this inventory to the attainment of the standards can emission trades be confidently seen as one avenue to attainment" (Tietenberg 1985: 119). EPA reformers, however, have insisted that the program would "promote faster compliance and better emission measurement since only quantified reductions below current requirements could be used to meet or avoid requirements elsewhere, [and would offer state] agencies a painless way to upgrade their inventories and correct other deficiencies on a gradual basis, as individual . . . applications arrived" (Levin 1982: 68). In response, opponents of emissions trading and incentive-based regulatory reform have argued that such approaches only provide polluters with greater opportunity to take advantage of the defects in the existing air quality management system to the detriment of air quality and human health.

Yet a third issue that has sparked disagreement over the implementation of emissions trading concerns how the "baseline" should be defined that will determine what emission reductions can be considered excess and therefore can be credited for use in emission trades. The baseline issue is complicated because it involves interpretations of both the Clean Air Act and EPA regulatory requirements. Proposals for a baseline definition have included using an existing administrative requirement such as RACT (Reasonably Available Control Technology), variations on RACT or other requirements, or using the emission levels historically associated with a given pollution source (Liroff 1986: 15–16). The debate over a baseline definition thus has involved arguments over whether to use "allowable" emission levels (defined by administrative requirements) as opposed to "actual" emission levels (defined by the historic pollution record of a source) in calculating credits for emission reductions.

Advocates of emissions trading have pushed for the use of administrative requirements to define baselines, contending that such an approach would provide pollution sources with a more flexible array of control options. This flexibility in turn would offer them a greater incentive to engage in trading and thus a greater incentive to find and exploit emission reductions. Finally, reformers argue, using an existing administrative requirement would provide insurance that air quality standards would be maintained.

The program's critics contend that baselines must be defined in terms of the actual emissions emanating from a source, especially when such emissions have historically been below what regulations have required. To do otherwise, opponents protest, would enable sources to create "paper" trades, in which the differences in emissions between those allowed by regulation and those actually emitted by a source, differences which exist only on paper, may be traded against real increases in emissions elsewhere. The result, some critics charge, would be real increases in emissions rather than the same level of air quality achieved at less cost. The baseline issue has ignited particularly heated exchanges because any given definition of baseline will have important impacts on both the pollution control costs of firms and the quality of the air in a region.

QUESTIONING THE PRACTICALITY OF INCENTIVE-BASED REGULATION

Disputes over the discretion and flexibility granted to states by the Clean Air Act, over the definitions of key terms in the Clean Air Act, over the reliability of SIPs, the definition of baselines, and a host of other disagreements have plagued the implementation of emissions trading and consumed a great deal of the energy and attention of the refomers in the agency. Part of this reflects a political strategy used by EPA staff opposing emissions trading and incentive-based reform. Program foes used the strategy to force legal and technical questions to the top of the emissions trading implementation agenda, thus focusing policy deliberations on areas in which the knowledge and expertise of reform opponents was greatest.[1] The agenda of the bubble concept task force, and the criteria it used to evaluate the bubble, clearly reflect the strategic maneuvers for shaping program implementation employed by opponents of emissions trading and incentive-based reform in the EPA.

More importantly, however, the extended list of conflicts over the implementation of emissions trading reflect basic questions about the feasibility of the program itself and the potential for employing incentive-based approaches to pollution control generally. Broad skepticism about whether incentive approaches for pollution control can work in practice is clearly evident in Congress's treatment of economic incentives (see chapter 3). EPA staff and other participants in the development of emissions trading also raised basic questions about the viability of emissions trading and related incentive-based regulatory reform ideas.

Concerns about feasibility were in part related to some of the implementation issues just discussed, especially the weaknesses in the existing air quality accounting system, including the poor quality of emission inventories and air quality modeling that is not well developed. Skeptics in the agency and among its principal clientele (and even among some supporters of incentive-based regulation) also questioned the range of applicability of emissions trading and related incentive techniques, contending that quasi-market arrangements would only work under certain limited conditions and only for a narrow set of pollutants, making the economic gains predicted by the theory of incentive-based pollution control much less impressive.

As one former manager in EPA's Office of Planning and Management explained,

> I think [incentive-based] program approaches are best designed to fit situations where you are attacking the problems for the first time. You don't have a lot of regulations getting in the way. . . . I think it's best in a situation where the physical characteristics allow you to keep track of that which you have permits for readily. The chlorofluorocarbon case was an ideal one because there weren't very many manufacturers of chlorofluorocarbons, it's very easy for the government to control the inventory, to know where they came from, how many there were, where the plant was, and so forth.[2]

At the root of this concern about workability, however, was considerable apprehension about whether emissions trading or any incentive approach could be administered effectively, and whether the advantages outweighed any new administrative burdens imposed. Disputes about the administrative practicability of emissions trading thus largely turned on questions about the resource demands and the increased complexity introduction of the program would impose.

For example, one implementation controversy involved the question of whether the "transition" costs for moving to emissions trading or a related incentive scheme would be too high. Skeptics argued that whether EPA merely grafted emissions trading onto the existing regulatory framework or made a more fundamental transformation of that framework, substantial resources would have to be invested in establishing new accounting procedures for tracking the creation, trading, and destruction of emission reduction credits (ERCs), the creation of emissions credit banks, and retraining of pollution control staff to administer such novel procedures, or the training of a new generation of pollution control "accountants." EPA staff working on the development of banking in connection with emission offsets realized early on that such transition costs had to be faced in moving to a quasi-market approach to pollution control, and this realization served to validate the transition costs argument put forth by EPA staff and others outside the agency keenly interested in the development of the program.

Opponents faced the difficulty of arguing over what was essentially an empirical problem, however. The reformers argued that transition costs would be minimal because emissions trading was merely a supplement to existing regulations. Moreover, the savings realized by society from the greater efficiency of an incentive approach would far outweigh the added costs of moving to a new system. Foes of the program, who argued that transition costs would far exceed the expectations of reformers, could not prove their point without the program first being put into place. The extent of the commitment of resources and the momentum generated by implementing emissions trading would serve as powerful arguments against canceling the entire endeavor even in the face of substantial new demands for resources to complete the transition to the new system. This catch–22 seemed to neutralize challenges to emissions trading based on concerns about the amount of society's resources that would be consumed in transition to a new regulatory framework.

EPA reformers saw a second dimension to the question of transition costs, however, and this dimension posed a much more formidable problem with which to contend. Program advocates realized that in moving to any incentive-based pollution control program, and thus away from direct regulation, even moving to a program as modest in its scope as emissions trading, would require modifying the behavior of all the actors in the system. Most of the actors presently in the system have of course become quite accustomed to command and control, and some have even developed strong vested interests in direct regulation. Adjustments in the behavior of the individual actors would have to be made in ways that would insure that the full advantages of emissions trading, including flexibility, efficiency, and technological innovation, could be realized. To the program's doubters, tactics for addressing this behavioral modification problem would be especially uncertain in their outcomes, and the ultimate resource burdens required to change the behavior of system actors could not be estimated and thus could not be planned for well.

Although this issue was hardly debated broadly, confined as it was to the attention of some members of the Regulatory Reform Staff and staff in the Air Programs office, reformers in the agency took the problem quite seriously, and considered it one of the most critical challenges to successful implementation of emissions trading. As one former RRS member who gave considerable thought to the problem argued, the challenge would not be surmounted easily.

[C]hanging people's behavior is very tough to do. Emissions trading is basically behavior modification . . . , but can you imagine all the thousands of people whose behavior has to be modified, in very radical ways, just to get a couple of state rules in place? But once it's there . . . the benefits are . . . huge. . . . The risks are . . . one black ball stops a million white balls, and any regulator or anyone who doesn't see that they can benefit from a change in the regulatory program will stop it dead.[3] So you need to modify so many people's behavior so they all vote in the same way that we want them to vote. That is excruciatingly painful and a time consuming job to do. It's very, very difficult. Furthermore, changes are threatening to people you never anticipate are players. It takes a lot of thinking in advance, "Who are the real players?"

As this former EPA official's observation also reveals, agency reformers did not regard the problem as intractable. The emphasis put on both marketing the program and getting the program out to regions and states, even with numerous contraints attached, were clearly tactics designed by program advocates as important steps in beginning the behavioral modification of the actors in the system.

Further illustrating the arguments about administrative feasibility underlying many of the struggles over the implementation of emissions trading were concerns, expressed by many state pollution control administrators and EPA staff sensitive to state concerns, that emissions trading would greatly increase the resource demands associated with administering the pollution control system. In other words, this concern focused not on transition costs but on operations costs.

Quite consistent with the basic arguments favoring incentive approaches to regulation, EPA reformers argued that society not only would realize important savings in pollution control costs through the efficiencies pollution sources could achieve under the program, but that added societal resources would be saved through administrative gains of various kinds, particularly through bureaucratic streamlining. Most agency reformers were adamant in their position that savings in administrative resources were possible. Many of them took a dim view of arguments about the added administrative burdens emissions trading would impose like that expressed by RRS Chief Michael Levin: "State agencies saw resource drains behind every rock . . . " (Levin 1982: 75).

The more moderate view taken by many reformers, as expressed by a member of the RRS, was that emissions trading would impose some additional administrative resource burdens initially, but that these would fairly quickly be more than offset by administrative savings that would be realized because of the incentive characteristics of the program.

It's clearly true that, at least in the beginning, you have higher costs to state agencies because they have to absorb slightly different skills because you're not dealing with standardized equipment. It takes more resources to figure out if what someone is proposing to do really is equivalent. That tends to be a short-term problem. There is a hump in the beginning which starts to disappear when you develop the skills to start writing and evaluating these kinds of permits exactly the way you evaluated the old kinds of permits. There also seem to be, and these are very difficult to quantify . . . , offsetting gains in several areas.

In spite of such arguments by program advocates, the dispute over operational costs and administrative resource burdens proved to be a particularly controversial implementation issue because with many of the program's adversaries this was a serious problem state agencies, and then eventually the entire regulatory system as well, had to plan for; it would not just work itself out. One EPA headquarters official, who later came to see emissions trading in a more positive light, summarized well the substance and depth of this concern about the increased administrative demands emissions trading would generate.

Then I also knew that it would be very difficult, if a banking type of operation would emerge . . . , for a bureaucracy such as a state government or local municipal government to operate one of these things. The administrative overhead would be tremendous to keep an accounting of all these emission trades—just the bookkeeping would be tremendous. I thought that was a very large social cost. . . . To do the job right there would be a large transference of the cost of control from the private sector to the public sector as we [EPA] had to run the market, as we had to enforce the agreements.

A final example of the basic focus on practicability characterizing the issues raised by the implementation of emissions trading were concerns about the potential increase in complexity emissions trading would add to the air pollution control system. Anxieties about increased complexity are related to concerns about resource burdens because any increase in complexity is likely to require additional resources for increased monitoring and feedback that provide additional information to regulators, to insure that standards are properly maintained in the face of greater complexity. But participants in the development and implementation of emissions trading were concerned about increased complexity as a separate and distinct issue, irrespective of resource demands, because of fears that a more complex regulatory system could not be administered competently. At the heart of the issue were questions about the ability of regulators to perform new and unfamiliar tasks, such as keeping track of all the emission trades that might occur in an air quality control region, estimating accurately the environmental impact of any given emissions trade (and the aggregate impact of all trades in a region), and estimating the equivalence of emission reductions and corresponding increases.

In advocating a change to incentive-based regulation, EPA reformers argued that the burden of direct regulation, in light of the increasing constraints on state pollution control agencies, was a crucial factor to consider.

How could EPA continue to insist on point-specific regulatory requirements that involved the most rather than the least cost for air quality compliance? How could it demand that state agencies—faced with shrinking budgets, growing developmental resistance, and hostile legislatures—continue to regulate more and more small businesses while cranking down further on previously regulated ones? (Levin 1982: 73)

Skeptics and opponents of emissions trading, noting the complexity of the program itself (15 pages of preamble, 7 pages of policy statement, and 21 pages of "technical issues" in its final version in the *Federal Register*), considered the reformers' argument a doule-edged sword. With state regulators facing substantial budgetary and other constraints, they asked, how could EPA and state regulators continue to implement adequately the substantial requirements of the Clean Air Act and EPA regulations and also operate a new program burdened by substantial legal and technical constraints of its own?

Beyond questions about increased complexity and attendant increases in workload in the face of numerous constraints on regulators, program foes raised questions about the manageability of the tasks regulators would be required to perform to administer a program like emissions trading. For example, skeptics asked, how will regulators be able to keep track of the negotiations over trade deals among firms in a region and verify the legality of each trade? To many individuals worried about the workability of the program, the demands of such tasks required knowledge of securities and exchange laws and brokerage skills for which pollution control administrators had no training. Hence those new tasks would clearly complicate the job of regulators. If the response was that other administrators with the requisite knowledge and skills would handle the securities and exchange aspects of emissions trading, opponents argued that such a solution would only add more bureaucracy to the administration of pollution control, thus dousing any claims about bureaucratic streamlining.

A second set of administrators responsible for regulating the securities and exchange aspects of emissions trading also raised questions in the minds of some EPA staff and state regulators about competing bureaucratic missions or objectives. For example, would the new administrators be more concerned with generating revenue and protecting the market in pollution securities than in protecting public health? Such questions are reminiscent of the concerns raised by Edmund Muskie during congressional debate over the use of economic incentives in pollution control. As one interested observer wrote, foreshadowing the professional conflict over organizational control in the EPA associated with the move to reform regulation by introducing economic incentives, "the notion that creating a tradable emissions market will somehow reduce the bureaucratic burden of regulation becomes a somewhat more, not less, tenuous proposition. . . . Implementing tradable emissions permits will create a new regulatory bureaucracy, in which a substitution of economists for lawyers and engineers will occur on a broad scale" (Willey 1982).

Closer to their own knowledge and skills, many state pollution control administrators, along with staff in EPA's Air Programs office, raised perhaps the most nettlesome implementation question for EPA's reformers. Emissions trading's critics asked, how could regulators verify emission reductions and establish with certainty the equivalence of reductions and corresponding increases for trades, if each transaction was essentially unique and sources could use such a greatly expanded array of methods to achieve reductions? This question, more than any other, raised the specter of unmanageable complexity in the administration of pollution control with emissions trading added to the system.

Consider the problem of verifying emission reductions under the emissions trading program, which gives pollution sources much greater flexibility in choosing the methods to achieve emission reductions. State regulators have come to rely on the installation of control equipment as an important tool in verifying emission reductions. That is, through occasional site inspections to make sure pollution control equipment is installed and working properly, regulators certify that a particular source has achieved the necessary reductions in emissions and thus is in compliance with applicable standards. Under emissions trading, however, sources would not necessarily be required to install specific pieces of control equipment or use any mandated technological approaches to achieve required emission reductions. Instead, the incentives in the emissions trading program are intended to encourage sources to use a wide variety of technological controls, manufacturing process changes, and an infinite variety of combinations of such strategies to achieve emission reductions and earn emission reduction credits.

This critical switch in the fundamental approach to achieving emission reductions, emissions trading's critics contend, raises questions about the ability of the current system to adjust. Will regulators be forced to require pollution sources to install continuous emission monitors, which for many pollutants are technologically infeasible? If continuous monitoring technology cannot be used in many circumstances, will regulators have to learn in detail numerous manufacturing processes in order to understand how process changes will result in emission reductions? Because plant operators' expertise is concentrated on the manufacturing processes in their plants, one can expect plant managers to be most creative in their solutions to the problems of achieving emission reductions by manipulating those manufacturing processes. That is a principal attraction of incentive schemes. But for any given pollution source, regulators will only know that the process changes plant managers make will achieve emission reductions and thus qualify a source for ERCs if the regulators: (1) accept the word of the operators of the source; (2) install some type of monitoring technology, which requires at least a periodic check, if not continuous observation; or (3) learn the manufacturing processes of a plant so that they can recognize how changes proposed by plant operators will affect emissions generated by the manufacturing process employed at the plant. Save for option one, program foes argued, the advent of emissions trading appears to guarantee increased complexity in the air pollution control system and an increased probability that mistakes will be made, increasing the risks to public health.[4]

Option one, self-reporting, offers its own version of increased complexity, in the view of many program skeptics. If the internal revenue system is any model, some type of random auditing procedure must be instituted to make self-certification of emission reductions a viable option in pollution control. Again, then, new procedures requiring new and perhaps unfamiliar skills must be developed and possibly a new set of bureaucratic tasks and people to carry them out must be established. And if the market in ERCs operates with the volume and scope envisioned by the most ardent advocates of emissions trading, a pollution auditing procedure may be put under the same strains presently being experienced by the auditing procedures used by the Internal Revenue Service.[5]

Finally, from the viewpoint of skeptics and opponents, the complex problem of verifying the equivalency of emission reductions and increases poses considerable difficulties for the existing system that would only be exacerbated by the full-scale use of emissions trading. Richard Liroff explains the equivalence problem with respect to two pollutants, particulates and volatile organic compounds (VOCs), by noting that the emission standards set for these pollutants often do not take into account the different degrees of risk to environmental quality and human health caused by different substances that can be classified as VOCs or particulates. Liroff goes on to point out that because existing conventional strategies to control VOCs and particulates mix so many different substances in undifferentiated fashion into the two large categories, it is difficult to judge precisely the environmental equivalence of control strategies (Liroff 1986: 41).

With the likelihood that sources will employ many new, unconventional control strategies under emissions trading, the equivalency problem only magnifies in impact, adversaries of the program insist. As one state pollution control official, effectively summing up the debates over complexity, observed:

[Emission trades] are much more complex to administer because each transaction is generally a unique transaction. It's not exactly like anything else that's happened before. . . . When you get into the area of unique emission reductions, giving individual credits for those and tracking the changes, this may appear simple. But in actual practice it gets to be very complicated. What is an emission reduction? Is it permanent? Is it paper? How do you know it's going to have the same impact? In all cases, the environmental impacts are not exactly the same. They may be more favorable or less favorable. . . . We're finding as we get further into [this] that trades we would have allowed a year ago, we won't countenance today because we're getting better able to measure individual impacts of a particular source's activities. When they change, then the impacts, if we allow somebody else to go up someplace else, are going to be much different. . . . [But] the air program for the most part doesn't have that level of sophistication in its analysis.

CONCLUSION

EPA's regulatory reformers have had their hands full in wrestling with the many problems of putting incentive-based regulation into practice. The legal, technical, and administrative objections to emissions trading raised by EPA staff, state regulators, and environmentalists have constituted only one front on which the agency's crusaders for reform have had to do battle, however. The characteristics of incentive-based regulation, and the fundamental organizational changes, those explicitly intended by reformers as well as those only implied by the nature of the reforms, that accompanied the concerted effort to introduce economic incentive ideas into the EPA and the programs it operates, sparked battles over emissions trading that in some ways presented much more dramatic challenges to the reform movement in the agency. A dissection of such controversies is the focus of the next chapter.

NOTES

1. This strategy also provided the means by which EPA staff holding to the agency's original governing ethos could introduce the basic values and ideas of their professional ideologies into policy deliberations over emissions trading. Ideological and philosophical dimensions of the policy deliberations concerning regulatory reform in the agency are explored in more detail in chapter 6.

2. Atmospheric research has revealed that chlorofluorocarbons (CFCs) have been collecting in the upper atmosphere and damaging the ozone layer, which screens out dangerous levels of the sun's ultraviolet rays. EPA proposed to control the manufacture and use of CFCs, the key chemical ingredient in many aerosol propellants and refrigerants, through either a "Mandatory Controls Approach" or an "Economic Incentives Approach." EPA dropped the economic incentives strategy in the face of substantial opposition from both industry and environmental groups. Many of the arguments against the economic incentives approach were quite similar to the implementation challenges administrators of the emissions trading program faced, as well as the philosophical objections explored in detail in chapter 6. See EPA (1980a) and Shapiro and Warhit (1983).

3. Arguments about vested interests and other disputes centering on "political influence" issues cannot be completely ignored in any analysis of the conflicts sparked by emissions trading. Other scholars studying policy development in the EPA, especially Marcus (1980b, 1982), have portrayed vested interests and political influence as critical elements in explaining the obstacles to the broader use by EPA of economic incentive schemes in its regulatory programs.

EPA's reformers saw the political and institutional resistance from vested interests, particularly in state agencies, as a serious implementation problem facing emissions trading. Many state administrators had a different perspective on the question, however. A number of state regulators argued that EPA pressure on state agencies to go along with an emissions trading program that was ostensibly voluntary only created more problems because it stiffened the resolve of some states not to participate actively and positively in the program. Many state agency personnel regarded EPA's reformers as intrusive, unyielding, insensitive to state concerns, and needlessly zealous about the program. In short, from the varying perspectives of participants in the development of emissions trading, the political influence problem could be seen as either a problem of vested interests in the status quo or federal intrusion and bullying.

4. Charles Perrow has conceptualized the problem program skeptics seemed to be referring to here as the "interactive" complexity associated with high-risk systems

that leads to "normal accidents." Perrow's research suggests that increasing inter-active complexity increases the chances that small failures will combine to create major accidents or "system accidents" even in competently administered systems (see Perrow 1986: 147).

5. One recent account describes the current plight of the Internal Revenue Ser-vice's audit system. "Tax audits are being performed at the lowest rate ever—12 per 1,000 compared with 20 per 1,000 in 1980. . . . [T]he IRS has even eased its secret standards or 'tolerance levels,' which determine how big a taxpayer . . . filing discrepancy it will pursue aggressively" (Sawyer 1985: 7).

6

IDEOLOGICAL CONTROVERSIES

The issues surveyed in chapter 5 illustrate the many challenges that have punctuated the implementation of emissions trading. Technical problems, legal protests, and basic questions about the prospects for the success of the program in practice provided more than enough fuel to fire substantial dissension and debate within EPA and the air pollution regulatory community. Nevertheless, an additional source of disaccord lay behind the controversy that engulfed emissions trading. Although implementation problems dominated the nominal agenda of emissions trading policy deliberations, peeling away the multiple layers of contention connected with a few of the most quarrelsome issues reveals the central terms of the conflict over emissions trading. The fundamental ideas at issue in the internal agency disputes tellingly reflect the nature of the political struggle that took place in connection with regulatory reform, a battle that was waged over the professional heart and soul of the agency.

Controversies regarding banking and the concept of surplus emission reductions in nonattainment areas, safeguards placed on the existing-source bubble, and the status of emission reductions generated by plant shutdowns, all had a direct bearing on the implementation of emissions trading. A close examination of each of these issues reveals, however, that beneath the quarrels over legality, technique, and administrative practice lay sharp ideological differences regarding the development of emissions trading and the introduction of incentive-based regulatory schemes into the national program for air pollution control.

BANKING OF SURPLUS EMISSION REDUCTIONS

Banking was crucial to the success of emissions trading, EPA reformers argued, because it would provide emission reductions when and where a source needed them. Without banking, a source seeking to modernize or expand would have to find a companion source willing to produce emission reductions at the right time and in the right amount. What made banking, and all of emissions trading, possible was the concept that surplus emission reductions in nonattainment areas were possible under the Clean Air Act.[1] The question of whether EPA and state pollution control agencies could create systems for banking surplus emission reductions generated by sources in nonattainment areas, was, therefore, first a legal issue. RRS Chief Michael Levin again provides the most useful description of the issue from this perspective.

To avoid prohibiting economic growth, EPA issued a 1976 "Offset Ruling" that allowed major modifications, expansions, or wholly new sources to construct in [nonattainment] areas so long as they installed very stringent controls and secured sufficient extra reductions from nearby sources to produce a net decrease in emissions. . . . This issue was a central point of EPA's internal debate during 1978, with the Air Programs and Enforcement staffs insisting *first*, that any such [approach] was illegal after ASARCO, and *second*, that every available reduction should be seized in nonattainment areas, regardless of its small size or high cost. (Levin 1982: 69–70, emphasis in original)

While the debate raged within the agency, environmental groups served as the outside point men in the legal battle against surplus reductions in nonattainment areas. The arguments of environmental groups like the Natural Resources Defense Council (NRDC) and Citizens for a Better Environment (CBE) best reflect the arguments program foes put forward in challenging the legality of the concept of surplus reductions in nonattainment areas. NRDC argued, for example, that "Treating reductions as surplus despite area-wide pollution deficits violates the Clean Air Act." Expanding on the argument, NRDC stated, "The states cannot properly declare some reductions 'surplus' and insulate them, even contingently, before identifying the necessary minimum measures for meeting their pollution reduction 'deficits' " (Ritts 1982: 28).

CBE-Chicago in turn argued, "EPA should not permit bubbles in areas lacking approved attainment demonstrations. [U]ntil the reductions needed can be identified, emission reduction credits cannot be regarded as truly surplus. They may be needed for attainment of the standards."

CBE-California asked, "Does EPA mean that only reductions in excess of those needed to meet ambient standards by the statutory deadline qualify for use in emission trades? If so, how can EPA sanction trades in nonattainment areas which do not have an approved plan which demonstrates attainment?" (Ritts 1982: 29). Summing up, CBE-California questioned EPA's rationale that without banking, "firms risk losing surplus reductions should a major SIP revision or new set of control requirements be instituted. . . . If a major SIP revision or new set of control requirements needs to be instituted the reductions were never surplus in the first place" (Ritts 1982: 95).

EPA found in the optional "growth allowance" approach to resolving the conflict between economic growth and air quality protection, which Congress provided in the 1977 Clean Air Act amendments, the statutory authority to allow banking of surplus emissions in nonattainment areas. Nevertheless, the controversy involving one of the pillars on which the emissions trading program was built extended beyond the narrow disputes over statutory interpretation. Banking of surplus emission reductions in nonattainment areas also raised fears about the failure of the air pollution regulatory system to make progress in cleaning the air and keeping it clean. At still deeper levels the banking issue revealed fundamental divisions within the EPA and among the principal interested parties outside the agency over the propriety of using the market as a public policy tool and the importance of maintaining clear distinctions between the public and private sectors of society.

The actual air quality impact emissions trading would have, if EPA's interpretation of the Clean Air Act allowing surplus emission reductions to be created and banked in nonattainment areas withstood the legal challenges, was a major bone of contention within the agency and among outside observers. Program advocates recognized the concern, but insisted that EPA's interpretation of the law—providing that surplus reductions could only be created when they did not interfere with progress toward attainment—and other regulatory safeguards designed into the program insured that air quality would be protected and improved where required. The assurances of reformers did not assuage the worries of skeptics and program critics, however. One private citizen, prompted by his local environmental advocacy group to respond to EPA's proposed Emissions Trading Policy Statement, framed the arguments of the opposition quite well. "Allowing one polluter to undo the good someone else has done . . . just maintains some fixed level of pollution which is considered tolerable. The banking system for extra reductions of pollution . . . which stores them for future sale really is not going to improve the air" (Ritts 1982: 6).

Quite consistent with this statement were the objections to emissions trading on grounds of air quality impact voiced by some EPA staff, state regulators, and environmentalists. The positions expressed by a member of EPA's Air Programs staff, and a state regulator, respectively, detail the nature of the objections.

[My] concern . . . was . . . this is just not right, it's certainly not promoting . . . continued progress toward attainment. . . . If anything, it could easily be viewed as an activity that would have . . . slowed up progress because . . . EPA would have been in effect approving [trades] based on a limitation which had no relation at all to what ultimately is required for attainment.

Baltimore [for example] had its first smoke ordinance in 1908. Since that point in time, pollution levels have dropped remarkably through the efforts of control programs, but primarily through the change in technology associated with producing a product. . . . If we come along [now] and establish a property right, then you don't allow the natural evolution of business to take place and reduce those levels of emissions, because you're establishing a fixed inventory, which then can theoretically repeat forever. . . . [T]he natural evolution of business toward cleaner products, which would occur anyway, would have produced lower levels of emissions than you, in government, will now allow. You are, in effect, preserving a higher than necessary level of pollution.[2]

Travelling deeper into the disputed territory surrounding banking and surplus emission reductions reveals that beyond questions about the air quality impact of emissions trading, supporters and opponents of the program held divergent views about the propriety of using the market to reach important public ends. Program advocates of course found the market an immensely practical instrument for accomplishing public objectives. What better way is there, reformers asked, to clean the air than to use incentives to harness the rational self-interest of individuals and firms in a market economy? Skeptics and foes of the program were much more dubious about the market as a suitable tool for attaining environmental quality and public health goals. This skepticism mirrored Senator Muskie's observation that using the market for cleaning the air and water was a very uncertain endeavor. A House committee staff person described the uncertainty issue in particularly colorful terms. Annoyed by the label "command and control" applied to the structure of the Clean Air Act, the staff person stated, "I have another label to throw on, which is 'shake and bake.' That's what the bubbles and offsets are, just a shake and bake program. You might get something on the chicken and you might not. You might get some chicken in the bag and you might not. The whole thing is so iffy that I have to worry about whether the public is being cheated."

An EPA headquarters staff person working in the administrator's office and generally sympathetic to reform voiced additional concerns about the market as policy instrument.

We need some type of control mechanism, whether it is technology or currency based, until efficiency is fully integrated into industry. . . . We need some kind of accounting system, but the problem is that people think ill of markets, and it is difficult for them to accept such an approach. . . . In the move from command and control to emissions trading . . . the real political . . . challenge is to protect the environment by avoiding the adverse environmental impact of concentrations of pollution from monopolies buying up the pollution rights.

Critics of emissions trading and its provision for banking surplus emission reductions, the key to establishing a market in pollution offsets, thus objected to the use of the market as a tool for environmental policy on two counts: (1) the market was too uncertain a device, with the implementing agency losing too much control over the activities vital to accomplishing public policy objectives; and (2) the market could not be trusted, because many of its qualities (and defects) made it ill-suited to public endeavors.[3]

To the extent that it is separable from objections to the market as too uncertain and uncontrollable a policy device, distrust of the market flows from arguments that the baggage that comes with the use of the market in public policy contains too many characteristics not properly suited to the pursuit of broad public aims. As the staff person in the EPA administrator's office argued, "there are inevitable limits such that it is never possible to achieve the purely free system." Hence the market is defective, for example, because monopolization and concentration of economic power is possible. Defects like these leave the market ill-suited for use in public policy. Others distrust the market as a policy tool because it encourages certain kinds of behavior, such as competition and calculativeness, not to mention avarice and greed, considered inappropriate for public pursuits.[4] Still others distrust the market as a policy instrument because it fails to take account of certain values many consider vital to properly designed public policies. The most important of these values is distributive equity. As Robert Levine (1972) has argued, market approaches are much less appropriate where major concerns about the distribution of resources are linked to a policy question.[5]

Needless to say, many of EPA's most ardent regulatory reformers found objections to the market as a policy tool unpersuasive. Advocates of emissions trading expected market-based techniques to achieve environmental goals more efficiently and effectively without compromising public policy objectives. They found most, if not all, the objections to the market raised by reform opponents ill-defined and easily dismissed through economic analysis. The objections to the market expressed by opponents of incentive-based regulatory reform were not based on any analytic rationale, however. The market as an object of uncertainty and mistrust flowed from basic ideas about what constituted an appropriate regulatory scheme, what institutions would be part of that scheme, and thus what techniques were most appropriate for achieving the ultimate goals for which regulation had been undertaken in the first place. This integrated view of regulation was built upon the professional ideologies and fundamental philosophical beliefs of program opponents. Emissions trading's supporters also held broad views of regulation and its place in the larger social and political system, albeit views that conflicted with the position held by the program's adversaries. These differing ideological views of regulation served to anchor the policy orientations and policy arguments of the combatants, and were at the heart of the controversy surrounding emissions trading.

Beneath the disagreements about the propriety of using the market as an environmental policy tool lay one more fundamental concern expressed by skeptics and foes of emissions trading. For some EPA personnel and outside observers, the use of incentive-based regulatory alternatives raised questions about the relationship between the public and private sectors of society. By introducing the market into efforts to achieve public objectives, they argued, it seemed that an implicit boundary between the public and private sectors was breached, and that important distinctions between public and private became unacceptably blurred. They suggested that by using the market as a regulatory device, administrative agencies somehow lost their "public-ness" and their place as part of a collective effort by society to reach collectively defined ends.

This worry over the blurring of the public-private distinction, a distinction that is already rather ill-defined in the American political economy, is not something to which the reformers in the EPA felt compelled to respond. The creed of EPA's regulatory crusaders clearly made "the public use of private interest" (Schultze, 1977) an acceptable, even preferred, strategy in the battle against public ills. But critics of emissions trading and incentive-based regulatory reform wondered whether the public use of private interest also meant the private use of the public interest. They wondered to how great an extent private parties would be able to use public resources to protect their private interests if the market became a widely used policy device. Granted this was not the stuff of extended or heated debate over banking or other aspects of emissions trading within the agency. It does demonstrate, however, that deep divisions between views about the roles and relationships of governmental and nongovernmental institutions were an important part of a number of conflicts fueled by the development of emissions trading and the broader movement for incentive-based regulatory reform in the EPA.

REGULATORY SAFEGUARDS AND THE EXISTING-SOURCE BUBBLE

EPA's January 1979 proposed bubble rule contained a series of restrictive conditions. For example, EPA allowed bubbles only in areas with approved SIPs projecting attainment, each emissions point included in a bubble required a specific emissions limit tied to an enforceable testing technique, and EPA allowed no delays in existing enforcement actions in connection with any bubble. This move to place a regulatory safety net under the bubble "reflected the tug-of-war within the EPA between bubble proponents and opponents. It indicated that the agency had decided to give great weight to concerns about enforceability . . . , even if it meant reducing the number of trading opportunities" (Liroff 1986: 42).

The internal agency combat over what regulatory safeguards should be attached to the bubble, as well as what safety mechanisms should be included in emissions trading generally, was the nuts-and-bolts expression of the most hotly contested question to arise out of the movement to bring in-centive-based regulatory reform to pollution control in the EPA: was emis-sions trading, or any form of incentive-based regulation, enforceable? Reform advocates and foes alike mentioned enforceability more frequently, and discussed it at greater length and in greater detail, than any other topic of debate during the course of the interviews undertaken for this study.

Fears that emissions trading would open the air pollution regulatory system to unprecedented abuse, manipulation, and gamesmanship by re-calcitrant polluters fulminated the enforceability debate. These fears about the greater potential for abuse and evasion of the law that incentive-based regulation would introduce into air pollution control, and anxiety about the inability of the existing enforcement mechanisms to compensate for what many saw as massive loopholes, impelled many state regulators, en-vironmental groups, and personnel in EPA's air and enforcement programs to oppose emissions trading. Comments from an environmental advocate and a former member of EPA's Office of General Counsel, respectively, reflect the views of opponents of emissions trading on the enforceability question.

We felt the bubble policy was going to be an invitation to chicanery. My personal view and I think it's shared [by] others is that what the bubble policy meant was more, and more complex, bureaucratic decision making in which the opportunities for either outright fraud or . . . hiding the ball for the bureaucrats to give away without being quite so obvious were multiplied.

I realized all the games that were played—legal maneuvers that were played through regulatory loopholes, legal loopholes, administrative procedure loopholes, and I saw this [emissions trading] as just widening any that were already there or adding a few huge ones to it.

In addition, an EPA regional official sketched a scenario for an enforcement breakdown under emissions trading that reflected the opinions of many of the program's foes.

I think . . . companies will delay compliance and finagle around with deals, . . . wait-ing not to comply, deferring a particular expenditure, and they won't comply. They'll say, "Well, [we] don't really want to comply with these RACT rules for [our] cinder plant . . . , [we'd] rather buy the emissions, but we're shopping around for the best price." They shop for two years. Then [they] say, "Well, [we] decided not to buy the emissions, everybody's prices are too high. [We're] going to go ahead and put on RACT. But it'll take [us] three years to put on RACT. [We've] got to get the money together, [We've] got to get all the engineering proposals. . . . " So you've got five years sitting there, with no clean-up.

Even some reformers in the agency acknowledged the validity of chal-lenges to emissions trading regarding the increased potential for manipulation and skirting of regulatory requirements the program would introduce into the air pollution control framework. One of the original designers of the program argued that

you need to have a very strong enforcement capability. . . . [T]his is why the environmental community has never been that happy with this whole stuff because . . . they have reason to believe that . . . these systems will be used to get out of regulations that they have fought for and we have certainly given them some reasons to believe that's what will happen.

Yet most reformers in the agency criticized the attacks on emissions trading with respect to enforceability as needless hysteria. One of the first administrators of the bubble policy stated, "I think there are areas where it's relatively easy to exploit the existing regulatory structure. . . . I think that some of those risks are real, but I also think imagining the devil behind every bubble application is also ridiculous."

Here was the crux of the matter. The devil crept into the confrontation over regulatory safeguards because such disputes as the one over conditions to be placed on the bubble revolved around fundamental differences in views about, first, the trustworthiness of industry, and second, pollution and pollution control as questions of ethics and morals.

Granted, not all opponents of emissions trading were driven to paint industry as veritable demons out to destroy the public's health by polluting the air. Some critics of emissions trading argued that because of the nature of pollution as an externality and because of the incentives and pressures pollution sources, mostly as private, profit-making companies, faced, incentive-based public policy just would not be sufficient to alter corporate behavior to favor the public interest. Sticks were more effective than carrots. The co-founder of an environmental litigation group expressed this view clearly.

I just think . . . people sitting in those chairs in corporations . . . often have very different views of what appropriate public policy is. But even if I sat in one of those chairs, the forces on me would be [the same]. . . . If I said, "Well, we're ready to clean up our mills because it's terrible. We can't go on killing people this way," the Board of Directors would be perfectly correct to say, "Yes, but why do *we* have to do it and if we do it, what is that going to do to our profits compared to our competitors?" They would make me answer, and they should because that's their job. So I don't put a lot of moral weight on it. I just think that's the nature of the institutions. . . . [T]hat means the government must command people one way or another to do what's in the public interest.

Many of the antagonists were driven to frame the dispute over regulatory safeguards for the bubble, and the general debate over command and control versus economic incentives, as black and white, however. RRS Chief Mi-

chael Levin in particular was sensitive to the moral and ethical coloration
to the debate over emissions trading, writing that "[environmental] groups
had helped draft the Clean Air Act not merely to clean the air, but to punish:
to force firms that for decades had used the atmosphere as a free dump to
pay the maximum amount for past sins" (Levin 1982: 65). Other reformers
in the agency described the motivations of emissions trading's adversaries
in similar fashion.

The biggest part of it is not trusting industry. There's just a philosophical objection
to somebody buying their way out of something. There is a feeling that our mission
is to put controls on each and every emission point. . . . I think it physically pains
many of these people—very competent people—that we might have a new plant
coming on line with less than the best available control technology. Never mind
that one immediately adjacent to it is overcontrolled. . . . The presence of that one
facility . . . is just painful.

Hence a deep distrust of industry, largely because it is unconcerned about
public health and the quality of the environment in the drive for profits,
was central to the views of program opponents about their mission: they
were to establish and maintain a regulatory system to keep industry from
doing bad things, like polluting the air, that industry could not otherwise
resist doing. A state regulator articulated that mistrust in no uncertain terms.

A regulatory agency is really an extension of the state's police powers. . . . That's
all we are—qualified cops. If you want to believe there is nobody going over the
speed limit . . . because they say they aren't, be my guest, but you're not much of
a cop if you do that. You've got to have hard factual evidence. . . . How many times
have you heard about economic statements and reports made by big industry down
in Washington? They tell their stockholders something and they tell Washington
something else. Two sets of books. What makes you think they wouldn't develop
two sets of books—one for the control agency and one for the stockholders? . . .
[Y]ou've got to protect [the system] so that all these charlatans that come along
don't get the best of you.

Beyond even the stark contrasts between advocates and foes of emissions
trading in their views about the trustworthiness of industry, as seen through
the dispute over regulatory safeguards in the bubble, lies a basic moral and
ethical dimension to the program conflicts. RRS Chief Levin's observations
touch upon this moral dimension. From the point of view of many opponents of emissions trading, especially in EPA's Air Programs and Enforcement offices, as well as among state regulators and environmentalists,
allowing firms to participate in a market in pollution, making pollution a
commodity and thus somehow legitimizing it, is wrong. Pollution is bad,
they say, the act of polluting is irresponsible, and it should be stopped
without qualification. Most of EPA's reformers recognized that some foes

of their program objected to incentive-based regulation on moral grounds. Nonetheless, like RRS Chief Levin, the reformers regarded most ethical objections to emissions trading with mild disdain. Undaunted, one committed foe of incentive-based regulation stated his case at length.

[T]he government cannot get into the business of marketing [pollution] to kill other people. I mean that's just morally . . . wrong and it's contrary to everything that this system—this country—is supposed to stand for. . . . I think what we've got to bear in mind here, we're talking about killing people and putting them in the hospital. If I were to kill somebody . . . or I were to put somebody in the hospital, there wouldn't be any hesitation on the . . . representatives of the public's [part] in tossing . . . me in jail. But somehow when it's a corporation. . . . [Y]ou know, Johns Manville almost literally murdered thousands of asbestos workers and we are standing around arguing about whether Johns Manville should be allowed to survive. There's no argument there. That's the most morally and socially reprehensible kind of behavior. Why in God's name we should allow people to kill other people merely because they happen to be corporate officers I cannot fathom.

Steven Kelman has explored this moral and ethical dimension to views about pollution control as part of his research into the question of why policy makers have been slow to put economic incentive ideas into practice. Drawing on his research findings, Kelman argues that incentive-based approaches emphasize results with little or no regard for the motivations of the actors involved. Ignoring the intent or motive behind social actions, Kelman suggests, alarms individuals who are concerned with the kinds of values society cultivates. Kelman cites the example of criminal law, where the requirement of *mens rea* (criminal intent) must be present for an action to be considered a crime. The presence or absence of criminal intent will carry great weight in determining how an individual's actions are finally adjudicated.

Those with the strongest moral orientation among emissions trading's critics might argue that therefore we need to be cognizant of the motives of polluters so that we can tell whether they are engaging in the egregious act of polluting the air out of ignorance, incompetence, or some dark purpose. If the motives of polluters resemble the last of these, then action to punish past sins may be appropriate. Moreover, critics might contend, altruism, volunteerism, and charity may not prove very effective in achieving policy goals. Yet a wholesale reliance on results with little regard for motive or intent raises concerns that highly regarded but fragile values like selflessness may be lost, while other values like selfishness, which are often criticized, proliferate.

Kelman concludes that each of us is concerned for the existence and production of certain societal values. That is, we are concerned about how people's preferences are formed and what those preferences are. This reflects our interest in the shape of society as a whole. Of course, society is more than an aggregation of individuals. It is a complex set of elaborate inter-relationships between individuals, groups, and formal organizations. We generally agree that voluntary exchange generated by self-interest ought to play a very large role in defining the type of society we have. Nevertheless, significant subgroups in society, for example the elderly and children, depend for their existence on other relationships, based on other motives and values. As the most strident moralists among emissions trading's foes might argue, a society that manifests no concern for the proper relations among citizens will soon not have any (see Kelman 1981: 32–44; also see Elkin and Cook 1985).

The evidence gathered in the present study expands on Kelman's findings by demonstrating that moral objections were also part of the internal EPA debate over emissions trading. Such evidence further reinforces the notion that within the EPA, efforts to reform regulation generated considerable friction because of fundamentally different views among EPA staff about how to define the agency's professional character and how EPA should carry out its mission.

CREDITS FOR THE SHUTDOWN OF OBSOLETE PLANTS

The final controversial issue arising out of the genesis of emissions trading to be given treatment here reveals additional dimensions to the ideological conflicts in the EPA arising from the push for incentive-based regulatory reform in the agency. This issue concerns reductions in emissions created by the shutdown of outmoded manufacturing plants and other pollution sources.

As an implementation issue plant shutdowns have been the focus of disputes over how properly to credit emission reductions in granting firms ERCs. Battles over plant shutdowns thus have been closely connected to the debate regarding what should be the baseline used to calculate extra reductions, and the conflict over what can be considered a surplus emission reduction in a nonattainment area. Liroff summarizes the implementation issues associated with sanctioning credits for plant shutdowns.

Critics of emissions trading argue that liberally granting credits for curtailments or shutdowns of factories near the end of their useful lives could reduce substantially the obligation of those building major new and modified facilities to employ advanced technologies and to minimize new emissions far into the future. . . . Critics also contend that, since most shutdowns would occur anyway for economic reasons, no ERCs to industry should be given for them; the cleaner air from the shutdowns simply should benefit the public. . . . Proponents respond that if regulators have not relied on reductions from such shutdowns in their local plans for attaining the ambient standards, then credits should not be denied. In their eyes, a pound of pollution is a pound of pollution, regardless of how it is eliminated from the air, and giving credits for shutdowns encourages earlier shutdown of older polluting facilities. (Liroff 1986: 16)

Beyond the complicated legal and administrative issues concerning baselines and surplus emission reductions raised by granting credit for emission reductions from plant shutdowns, lay a host of questions about, first, the impact such credits would have on property rights, and second, the implications creating a valuable property right in air resources has for questions about distributive equity.

A sampling of the large number of comments submitted in response to EPA's proposed Emissions Trading Policy Statement (see Ritts 1982) gives something of the flavor of the controversy surrounding shutdown credits and property rights as seen from the eyes of EPA's principal clientele. The Natural Resources Defense Council argued, for example, "credit should be valid only for a period a source would have operated otherwise. This principle of 'temporal equivalence'—that reductions should last as long as the increase they balance . . . should be applied to control measures or curtailments [as well as] shutdowns" (Ritts 1982: 41). The essence of NRDC's argument is that credits for plant shutdowns, or credits for any extra emission reduction for that matter, should not have an infinite lifetime, because this creates a property right in air resources wholly unconnected to the reasons the reductions are created in the first place.

A number of commentators supporting emissions trading opposed concepts such as temporal equivalence because, they contended, conditions placed on the property right created by ERCs would limit the economic value of credits and thus dilute the incentives emissions trading offers to pollution sources to seek emission reductions and engage in trading activity. The American Petroleum Institute argued that the economic advantages of credits with little or no time limits attached "could be significantly reduced if a short time limit is established for banked ERCs, especially when major reconstruction or expansion is uneconomic under existing economic conditions" (Ritts 1982: 106). Likewise, the Utility Air Regulatory Group (UARG) argued, "Long time limits give sources more certainty that they will benefit from their banked emission reductions." If time conditions are imposed on credits, UARG argued, "utilities and other sources will be reluctant to close existing sources if they risk losing credit for their reductions by depositing them in the bank" (Ritts 1982: 107).

Numerous industries and utilities likely to benefit economically from a liberal EPA policy regarding credits from shutdowns, and the operation of the emissions trading program generally, also expressed concern about threats to their rights of property in pollution credits posed by government confiscation to meet additional needs for emission reductions, and from nonindustry groups seeking to buy up credits as a way to reduce emissions further than the law requires.

The Chemical Manufacturers Association argued that EPA's suggestion to states and localities that they may consider reserving ownership in certain classes of ERCs to themselves "could be read as an invitation to states to deprive sources of valuable emission rights without compensation" (Ritts, 1982: 101). Middle South Services, an electric and gas utility, stated, "we are concerned that a state could mandate deposits of any actual reductions regardless of cause and thus in part deprive the makers of the reduction of the direct benefit of the reduction without their consent" (Ritts 1982: 102).

Other industry and utility commentators wanted to restrict the property rights in pollution credits to "users." Jersey Central Power and Light argued, for example, that "ERCs should be owned only by the source which creates them unless the owner is paid the fair market value for the right of ownership" (Ritts 1982: 100). The Flexible Packaging Association urged EPA and the states to prevent nonusers, including environmental groups, foreign industries, and government bodies, from purchasing ERCs in order to protect the security of emissions credit banks. The Department of the Interior expanded on this argument about the need to limit who could hold property rights in pollution credits by urging EPA to consider the consequences of "outside" interests owning air resources.

In cases where it is not prevented by State regulation, it may be possible for Federal, State, or local governments or special interest groups . . . to purchase ERCs to preclude development in an area. These same entities could also sell ERCs to promote development in an area. In effect, future economic growth and development of an area could be controlled by certain "outside" entities or interests. (Ritts 1982: 102)[6]

Other commentators held markedly different perspectives on the question of who should own the rights to resources and what the implications for such ownership would be. An Oklahoma county health department argued that emissions trading "would seem to transfer ownership of air resources from the citizens to the corporations. This is in direct conflict with the philosophy of the state and local governments. We view these resources in the same light as water resources" (Ritts 1982: 4). The Wisconsin Department of Natural Resources expanded on this theme. The department's comments encapsulate much of the debate about property rights that took place outside the agency. They deserve quotation at length.

We seem to be rapidly turning the assimilative capacity of the environment into what may eventually become a very valuable property right as a result of this policy and other associated regulations. At the same time we are giving this new property right away with little cognizance on the part of the public as to the ramifications of this action. A few private entities could hold the economic future of an area in their hands because of their control of the assimilative capacity for various emissions. This country has already gone through giveaway[s] of this type in the distribution of water rights in the west and grazing rights on public lands. It would seem intelligent to try to learn from these lessons. (Theiler 1982: 5)

Debate over property rights surrounding emissions trading, evident in these comments from EPA's principal clientele, was carried on within the agency as well. Economists and other advocates of economic incentives in pollution control have always been unhappy with the whole "license to pollute" issue that has dogged proposals to use incentive-based regulatory programs. The comments of Baumol and Oates are typical.

One of the most persistent arguments against fiscal incentives is the assertion that pollution taxes (or the auctioning of pollution permits) are basically immoral. Many environmentalists contend that a pollution tax is, in effect, "a license to pollute"— that whoever is willing to pay a price can abuse the environment. . . . Society has been giving away free too many of its precious resources far too long. It is not scandalous to decide that everything has its price; the real scandal lies in setting that price at zero or at some token level that invites us all to destroy these resources. . . . Unless we recognize the legitimate role of price incentives for the control of pollution, we may end up with our sense of morality intact but our environment the worse for continued abuse. (Baumol and Oates 1979: 244–245)

The attitudes of many EPA reformers were in tune with this position. As RRS Chief Levin has argued, environmental groups have used "right to pollute" or "license to pollute" criticisms of incentive-based regulation as a "shibboleth," or code phrase, intended to incite controversy (Levin 1982). A state regulator supportive of incentive-based regulation put it more bluntly. "I think it's a straw man argument. We give . . . property rights all over the place in the form of permits. They are licenses to pollute— that's all they are. It doesn't bother me; that's just recognizing reality. I think it's a nonissue. . . . It just doesn't impress me."[7]

To many critics and foes of emissions trading and incentive-based reg-ulation, however, concerns about the property rights implications were legitimate and deserved reasoned consideration. Attempts by some EPA reformers to slough off the property rights question as a minor issue only intensified the controversy. Comments from a member of EPA's Enforce-ment office, a state regulator, and a Senate committee staff person indicate the range of concerns about the property rights implications of emissions trading expressed by many of the participants in the program development process.

To control a thing called emission rights, . . . leads you to the fact that someone owns something that can attach a certain value that could in fact be traded or sold. . . . [T]he idea of creating a right or creating a commodity that can be bought and sold, [begins] to get into an area that I [feel] very uncomfortable about.

I think one of the principal questions is whether or not you are creating property rights in creating emission reduction credits. . . . [Property is] permanent, real, it's there forever and . . . being . . . the only thing tangible that people deal with in the law, the kinds of law that deal with property are unique. . . . Certainly unique to regulatory control programs. . . . [D]espite the fact that the law clearly says that this emission reduction credit will disappear after five years, 10 years, whatever . . . that's a lot of baloney, because regardless of what the law says or doesn't say, the evolution of property rights occurs because of case law and people challenging that kind of right. All you have to do is generate the property and . . . it has a life of its own despite law. So a peddler's license is a good example, a liquor license. They achieve value even though it is a licensing procedure. You try to take it back, you can't.

That phrase "right" is a critical one—right to pollute. There is no such thing as a right to pollute. . . . If it's legal, if as a society we're going to sanction the injuring of other people because it costs too much to avoid that, why . . . can't we take other things because it's too expensive to avoid injury . . . whether that happens to be a right of a trial by jury or a right of speech or a right of assembly or a right of religion or whatever it happens to be?

Kelman is again instructive in sorting out what is at the heart of the philosophical debate over property rights that lies behind the controversy concerning credits for plant shutdowns and, generally, markets in pollution rights. As Kelman explains, incentive-based regulatory programs raise the fundamental issue of how value ought to be assigned to social objects. Kelman points out that the market is not the only mechanism society uses to assign value to social objects. A nonmarket sector exists, for example, because society wishes to keep some precious objects out of the market to protect them from the cheapening or "downvaluation" effect of economic value (Kelman 1981: 69–72). In other words, by putting a price on objects that previously were assigned no economic value, such objects are, paradoxically, devalued.

Moreover, Kelman contends, society purposely keeps some precious objects out of the realm of the market because the value of these objects is of a different character from economic value. It is one thing to say, for example, that firms have the right to use a portion of the assimilative capacity of the atmosphere to produce goods and services of benefit to society, and that individuals have the right to consume the air for the life-sustaining oxygen it contains. It is quite another thing to define those rights as commodities by creating a market for them. Clearly by valuing those rights in economic terms, the character of the values changes, if in no other way than that the value of the firm's right is now greater than the right of the individual because the firm is willing, and able, to pay a higher price for its air right than is the individual, price being the only value yardstick available in the market.

As Kelman explains, society places the label "priceless" on objects like air and water resources, human life, and freedom to give them special status and thus special attention and treatment from government. It is in this sense that many critics of emissions trading argued that the program also raised questions about who ought to own objects valued by society. Many objects labeled priceless are of special status and thus in the public domain. In the United States, the public trust doctrine came into being to maintain the special status of environmental objects by identifying the government as trustee of natural resources. As trustee, government has the responsibility to insure that protected resources not be assigned to private use or that the public's interest in a resource not be limited (see Sax 1970). As some of the strongest critics of emissions trading argued, privatizing decisions about the final disposition of objects protected by the public trust doctrine is expressly prohibited. Yet, these critics argued, emissions trading does place in private hands decisions about the disposition of an irreplaceable natural resource.

Hence foes of emissions trading attacked the program on the grounds that it creates valuable private rights in a scarce public resource. Moreover, policy makers skeptical of emissions trading, but not necessarily wholly opposed to the program, at least questioned the extent to which agency reformers took cognizance of the property rights implications of their program. The debate over the property rights implications of emissions trading was fundamentally, therefore, a clash between program proponents and opponents in their views about how value ought to be assigned to objects in society, and who ought to own certain valuable objects.

This clash of basic philosophies between the two camps in the agency, and in the various groups outside the agency who participated in the development of emissions trading, stretched to one further field of battle that deserves attention. Because, from the perspective of many program participants, emissions trading would create new, fairly clearly defined property rights in air resources, both supporters and opponents raised numerous questions about how those valuable property rights would be distributed, especially in terms of the initial distribution of the rights, but also in terms of what conditions or limitations would be placed on who could hold such rights, how many they could hold at any one time, and how long the rights could be held, that is, the tenure of the rights. As one EPA enforcement official stated, "[I'm concerned about] the ethics of it. How do we go about determining who has the right? Does everyone have the right? Do just the largest polluters or those with the biggest assets? I'm concerned about equal opportunity of access to land, water, and air for everyone."

EPA's reformers also struggled with questions about how best to distribute the rights, not necessarily coming up with satisfactory answers. Two of the agency's key emissions trading decision makers provided instructive descriptions of the problems the program faced regarding questions about distributive equity.

Under the marketable permits concept you would have an auction . . . and equity would be based on ability to pay. That concerns me. You know, its not a whole new ballgame. There are existing firms out there with existing costs of control and existing roles in society and now [we] come in and impose . . . where do you start is the problem. Are you going to say, "Look, tomorrow we're going to have this auction and no one is grandfathered in"? So that's the fundamental problem I always see with marketable permit programs. I do think that small firms would be at a decided disadvantage and that's a problem we've always faced in terms of just buying and selling emission reduction credits. How do we help the small firms compete?

You have to allocate the permits or credits somehow. Do you allocate them by auction or do you allocate them by giving . . . most of them to the historical producers and consumers . . . ? If you auction them off, you learn how valuable they are. The control costs . . . , the direct regulatory costs of control . . . [are] less than half of the regulatory approach because of the efficiency of using them. However, the cost of buying the permits under an auction system would be much higher than the control costs of this traditional approach. That's because of the value of the rights to use these things in a restricted market. How do you convince industry to go along with this very efficient regulatory approach which ends up costing them twice as much . . . , a great deal more than the straight regulatory approach? Well you can't ever convince them of that. You have a big political fight on your hands. Now let's suppose for a moment that to get around that political fight because it is so strong you compromise with your pure principles and allocate along some historical grounds, recognizing the inefficiencies of doing so. What you're really doing is giving wealth to these companies . . . and giving away an awful lot of money for the companies because they happen to be the ones that were [around] at the time you started to regulate. . . . You are conceptually taking away wealth from the potential future entrants [into the market] unless you devise a method . . . to make some [of the credits] available in the future. And if you stop to think about it you're doing exactly the same thing when you regulate . . . if you design the regulation around . . . the present performance of polluters.[8]

The differences between advocates and foes of emissions trading on the question of how properly to distribute the valuable property rights created by the operation of the program, and how properly to distribute the benefits derived from possession of those rights, boiled down to basic differences in definitions of equity. Agency reformers and other program supporters tended to define equity in economic terms. For example, they criticized the existing command-and-control framework on grounds that it violated the economist's criteria of vertical equity—where unequals should be treated unequally and regressive patterns of distribution should be avoided—and horizontal equity, where equals should be treated equally. Program advocates contended that command and control forces all pollution sources within large classes to undertake the same pollution control strategy, irrespective of whether the costs of that control strategy varied widely across sources within a given class. By encouraging cost sharing through exchange of emission reduction credits, they argued, emissions trading provides a more equitable distribution of the financial burden of control among sources (see Tietenberg 1985: 122).

Advocates of emissions trading also tended to define equity in terms of efficiency. That is, what is most efficient is most equitable. EPA's reformers argued that the market in emission reduction credits would distribute control responsibility according to the differential costs of control. The incentives of the ERC market would encourage those sources that could control emissions most cheaply to assume the greatest control burden, with fewer resources consumed to achieve the same level of air quality. In short, the greatest control burden would be assumed by those sources with the lowest costs of control. Of course, economies of scale should be taken into account, meaning that some larger firms would be able to reduce their control costs through economies of scale in control equipment acquisition, installation, and operation that smaller firms would not be able to achieve. The distributional consequences for the benefits of operating in a system with emissions trading then fall right in line. Those firms assuming the greatest burden of emissions control would acquire the lion's share of ERCs and the valuable property rights in air resources attached to them.

In contrast, skeptics of emissions trading, and especially its most ardent opponents, tended to define equity in the terms of the traditional program approach, that is, as equal treatment. This definition means that every pollution source within a class of sources is required to meet the same technological standards and thus assume an equal share of the emissions control burden. If emissions trading was going to proceed, program foes insisted, the distribution of the property rights had to be based on some version of equal treatment, that is, each source within a class of sources would get an equal share of the rights. To allocate the rights on the basis of efficiency, or by some standard of historical use, emissions trading's critics continued, could invite economic and environmental blackmail.[9]

Once again, then, sharply divergent philosophical views about a concept critical to an important area of public policy, the proper definition of equity to use in devising pollution control programs, proved to be at the root of differences between supporters and opponents of emissions trading regarding an important implementation question. In this case the question concerned the distributive consequences of the program, and the differing professional ideologies of the parties involved again contributed to the contrasting positions on an issue crucial to the organization and operation of a regulatory system.

CONCLUSION

The chief of EPA's Regulatory Reform Staff, Michael Levin, in reflecting on his experience with implementing the bubble policy, has written, "major reforms are a combination of grass-roots organizing and trench warfare; to succeed, they require tenacity, expanding resources, constituency building, intimate knowledge of messy program details, and constant vigilence" (Levin 1982: 92). Through a survey of implementation issues, and through close scrutiny of three especially controversial issues associated with the development of emissions trading, I have tried to convey the essential substance of the struggle that took place in the EPA over regulatory reform, a struggle that forced Levin into administering the reforms with an attitude resembling that of a general administering a conquered province.

What remains to be done in this study is to put the pieces of the puzzle together to present a final picture of the impact regulatory reform has had on an administrative agency. That picture must link the professional conflicts and the ideological clashes over emissions trading with the organizational change strategy employed by reformers in the agency to bring incentive-based regulation fully into practice. To be complete, the final picture should consider the implications a powerful movement for regulatory reform has for bureaucratic politics, organizational leadership, and policy decison making in administrative agencies.

NOTES

1. The concept of surplus emission reductions in *attainment* areas, that is, areas already meeting all the ambient standards, is also necessary for banking to work. This concept generates little or no controversy, however, because in attainment (or PSD—Prevention of Significant Deterioration) regions, any emission reductions not needed to maintain the ambient standards are by definition surplus.

2. As this second excerpt suggests, concerns about the air quality impact of emissions trading ranged far beyond the issue of banking and surplus emission reductions in nonattainment areas, subsuming questions about property rights and a host of other issues. What I call ideological and philosophical concerns about the implementation of emissions trading thus are quite tightly intertwined. Individuals interviewed for this study raised such basic issues in a wide array of contexts and in association with a variety of implementation issues. Admittedly then, the manner in which I have categorized philosophical objections to emissions trading and have linked them to important implementation issues is somewhat artificial. My method does provide a way, I believe, to simplify the presentation and explanation of these complex issues. The section on credits for plant shutdowns that follows later in the chapter takes up an analysis of questions about property rights.

3. Arguments about the uncertainty and lack of at least apparent control inherent in the market as a policy instrument are strongly linked to the resistance in Congress to endorse economic incentives in pollution control (see chapter 3). Congressmen feared that they would not be able to retain sufficient control of the environmental policy apparatus should they allow administrators to introduce market elements into the air pollution regulatory system.

4. Concerns such as these also came to the surface in disputes over the safeguards

to be applied to the bubble policy, and are explored in more detail there. Also see Kelman (1981: 54–83) on this topic.

5. Concerns about distributive equity surfaced in connection with disagreements over how to credit reductions from plant shutdowns and the property rights implications of emissions trading. The third section of the chapter takes up an examination of these issues. Also see Kelman (1981: 84–86) on this topic and the expanded discussion in chapter 7.

6. Oppenheimer and Russell (1983) argue that the scenarios in which special interest groups, especially environmental groups, enter pollution rights or pollution credit markets, purchase the rights or credits, and "retire" them to lower emissions in an area below what regulations require have little basis in reality. The authors explain that no environmental group has sufficient capital to afford the market prices at which the rights or credits would likely be bought and sold.

7. Despite their rejection of right-to-pollute objections to economic incentives, economists interested in promoting wider use of incentive schemes in environmental regulation have explored property rights questions extensively. A good example is Tietenberg (1974).

8. The observations of this former EPA manager, an economist by training, reveal that economists have also directed their attention toward distributive issues raised by incentive schemes. Quinn (1983), Hahn and Noll (1983), and Tietenberg (1985: chapter 5) are representative examples. Hahn and Noll, for example, in examining data from extensive modeling of sulfur oxide emissions control for the Los Angeles basin using a tradable emissions permit system, argue that the existing property rights granted by issuing permits under the present air pollution control system act as barriers to reform toward a market system for permits. The substantial wealth attached to these existing permits is, they contend, "probably much greater than the efficiency gains that could be captured by allowing these permits to be fully tradable" (Hahn and Noll 1983: 71). Polluters thus have little incentive to enter into a market where their financial gains from efficiency are less than the wealth losses they suffer through redistribution stimulated by market trading of the permits. Moreover, this is precisely the sort of negative distributional outcome that led to stiff industry opposition to EPA's proposed "Economic Incentives Approach" for controlling chlorofluorocarbons (see Shapiro and Warhit 1983).

9. Tietenberg finds such market power and extortion scenarios unlikely.

Though in general the approach taken by the EPA in the emissions trading program has made market power more likely than necessary, the degree to which this manipulation could interfere with the basic objectives of the program seems small.... Should local control authorities become concerned that a unique circumstance in their trading area has created the threat of market power, the control authority could use its eminent domain authority to purchase... credits by providing just compensation.... The control authority could then sell the credit to some new source at a price which was sufficient to cover its costs (including administrative costs). (Tietenberg 1985: 145)

7

ORGANIZATIONAL CHARACTER AND POLICY REFORM

For nearly its entire history, the Environmental Protection Agency has been plagued by what Alfred Marcus calls "divided bureaucracy." A senior EPA official during the Carter administration, reflecting on the agency's experience with incentive-based reform, observed during an interview:

One side was this kind of intellectual side that favored these approaches and worked on getting them done. And the other side, . . . I considered much more macho, kind of, "God damn it, we'll clean up the lakes!" That sort of thing. . . . I think there were just two sides and there were two kinds of people in the agency so there [were] always these struggles for the soul, the heart, and mind of the administrator.

Students of environmental policy offer varying interpretations of the internal divisions that are part of the bureaucratic character of the EPA. Marcus (1980b), for example, traces a bifurcation in views about agency mission among EPA professional staff to the founding of the agency. He argues that the novel design of the EPA, with a single administrator and close accountability to both the president and Congress, differs substantially from the regulatory commission model. The latter provides for a more deliberative board or commission policy-making structure, substantial policy autonomy, and, most importantly, protection from direct presidential or congressional interference. In contrast, Marcus argues, the White House and Congress have more direct control over EPA actions. Consequently, the two branches have pulled the agency in separate directions from the very beginning. In Marcus's view, the perspective that drove the White House's formal proposal for a pollution control agency diverged sharply from the perspective that drove Congress's decisions about the policies it would give the new agency to implement. "For the White House, the objective was managing the environment comprehensively and achieving efficiency in making pollution reductions. For Congress, the goal was to

make rapid progress with respect to specific pollution control problems"
(Marcus 1980b: 78).

The result, Marcus insists, was the creation of a bureaucracy split along
policy versus program lines (the response to the system in its entirety exhibited by the White House versus the response to single parts of the system
exhibited by Congress). Marcus describes how conflict between presidential
and congressional policy intentions became imbedded in EPA's structure.

The White House was concerned about the conflict between environmental objectives and other national priorities. Those who had a policy perspective reflected
White House thinking in the agency and provided the evidence and arguments EPA
needed to justify its decisions when challenged by the White House. . . . Those with
a policy perspective were found mostly in the Office of Planning and Management.
. . .
   Most bureaucrats had a program perspective rather than a policy perspective. The
great bulk of bureaucrats were program managers and operators. . . . They took
their cues from Congress and reflected the fragmented nature of the legislative branch
which passed separate pollution control laws and amended them according to different principles. (Marcus 1980b: 107–108)

Bruce Ackerman and William Hassler (1981) offer a similar perspective
on the divided bureaucracy within EPA. The authors also start from the
premise that the organization of the EPA represents a new approach to
regulation. Ackerman and Hassler argue that in response to some of the
excesses of the commission model of regulation, first fashioned during the
late 1800's with the establishment of the Interstate Commerce Commission
(ICC) and used to its full potential during the New Deal, Congress attempted to go "beyond the New Deal" in the design of the EPA.[1]

For example, to increase accountability to the political branches, Congress
designed EPA with a single administrator, rather than the more deliberative
and pluralist board or commission. The administrator serves at the pleasure
of the president; that is, he does not have the protection of tenure that
extends beyond the four years of the presidential term. The EPA administrator must also be confirmed by the Senate. In addition, Congress placed
the EPA within the normal bureaucratic hierarchy, albeit separate from any
cabinet department, rather than independent of the normal framework as
with most New Deal regulatory commissions, thus giving the president
even more direct control. Finally, Congress organized the EPA to avoid
the greatest boogeyman of the commission model of regulation: clientele
capture. Although the ICC might be captured by the railroads or, later, the
trucking industry, the Federal Communications Commission might be captured by the broadcast industry, and the Atomic Energy Commission (now
the Nuclear Regulatory Commission) might be captured by the nuclear
power industry, EPA would not suffer the same fate. The agency would
encompass opposing clientele: environmentalists on one side and industry

on the other. This arrangement, Congress decided, would allow EPA to fend off capture by one set of clientele with the aid of a vigilant opposition.

Ackerman and Hassler find the approach of going beyond the New Deal in social regulation, as embodied in the design of the EPA, dubious at best. The design, they contend, allows the legislative branch too much control over administrative decision making. Congress draws itself into making technical decisions beyond its competence. The authors argue that the EPA model supplants bureaucratic expertise and technocratic rationality with the pulling and hauling of interest-group politics that characterizes the legislative process. The results are, first, an administrative process deficient in expertise, second, a process exploited for narrow interest-group purposes, and, ultimately, bad environmental policy.

Ackerman and Hassler find the intrusion of politics into a disabled administrative process, associated with Congress's revisions in the New Deal model of regulation, reflected in the bureaucratic struggle surrounding EPA's attempt to implement changes to section 111 of the Clean Air Act (New Source Performance Standards) passed by Congress in 1977.

Almost immediately, the EPA found itself divided along lines that reflected Congress's problematic attempt to move beyond the New Deal. On one side, the Office of Air, Noise, and Radiation (Air Office), run by Assistant Administrator David Hawkins, viewed Section 111 in political terms. From this view . . . it was wrong for an administrative agency to deny political activists the fruits of their congressional victory.

On the other side, the Office of Planning and Management (Planning Office), headed by Assistant Administrator William Drayton, represented the technocratic view. This office is composed principally of economists and policy analysts professionally predisposed to considerations of cost-effectiveness. They saw . . . [that] the statutory language—in contrast with the legislative history—made it clear that the administrator must take "into account the cost of achieving . . . emissions reduction" [sic] before imposing *any* requirement under Section 111. (Ackerman and Hassler 1981: 79–80, emphasis in original)

Richard Liroff offers another perspective on the divergence of views about environmental regulation evident within the EPA and reflected in agency actions with respect to the bubble policy and emissions trading. Liroff labels the two major camps in the agency "command minimalists" and "command expansionists." He identifies the command minimalists as "primarily officials on EPA's Regulatory Reform Staff," and command expansionists as including "officials in EPA's air programs office and environmentalists in organizations like the Natural Resources Defense Council" (Liroff 1986: 11).

Liroff's minimalists and expansionists hold sharply contrasting views about what is needed to fix the flaws in the command-and-control system for air pollution control established under the Clean Air Act. Command minimalists believe that reforms like emissions trading are important tools for overcoming the flaws in the existing system. For these tools to work, the minimalists argue, regulators must circumscribe command and control by defining " 'stopping points'—regulatory requirements they will not tighten" (Liroff 1986: 11). These stopping points provide a regulatory base on which industry can rely, and which will give polluters the incentive, particularly through emissions trading's ERC market, to identify new, more cost-effective abatement options. The results will be greater efficiency and better progress in cleaning the air and keeping it clean.

Command expansionists, on the other hand, argue that emissions trading and related reforms will only exacerbate the weaknesses of the existing system. Expansionists contend that overlaying the existing framework with emissions trading only opens up loopholes that industry can exploit to the detriment of the breathing public. Expansionists insist that the flaws in the air pollution control system must be repaired *before* emissions trading and related incentive-based reforms are fully operational. Expansionists suggest that EPA can close loopholes most effectively by making the operating rules for emissions trading fairly strict, that is, more like command and control.

THE MISCHIEFS OF FACTION

For most of the organizational life of the Environmental Protection Agency, then, the agency has operated with a fundamental schism in its professional ranks regarding views about the agency's mission, about the proper organization and purpose of a regulatory system, and about the appropriate instruments for achieving environmental policy objectives. The divergent views about agency mission, regulatory organization, and policy instruments reflect key differences in education, training, and ideological orientations between line and staff offices, especially between the Office of Policy Planning and Evaluation, as it is currently titled, and the Air Programs and Enforcement offices.

These very fundamental differences among both political appointees and career staff in the agency translated into distinctly different images of the organizational basics that should shape how the EPA went about its business. The attorneys and environmental engineers, who formed the professional core of the agency at its inception, insisted on organizational basics grounded in legal reasoning, emphasizing vigorous enforcement of pollution control laws and stern punishment for recalcitrant polluters.[2] Theirs was the image that dominated the bureaucratic character of the agency from 1970 to the inauguration of Jimmy Carter. In contrast, a much smaller band of economists and policy analysts, with ties to the environmental policy intentions of the Nixon White House—but who did not gain significant influence over policy making in the agency, despite being in charge of regulatory review, until the Carter administration took control—envisioned an organization and policy decision process anchored in economic reasoning, and emphasizing efficiency and a concern for the costs of environmental regulation.[3]

EPA could maintain a single governing ethos, emphasizing pollution control by rules and standards and enforcement by the adversarial legal system, and keep a significant challenge to the dominant professional ideology at bay, only so long as the influence of economists and policy analysts in policy deliberations remained circumscribed. Once the bureaucratic seal around the staff holding a vision of environmental regulation shaped in accord with a technocratic ideology, stressing efficiency and the use of economic analysis, was broken, professional conflict over policy and organization was inevitable. In a very real sense, the regulatory reform movement, brought to the agency by the Carter reformers, broke that seal.

Champions and Change Agents

The reformers who were already serving in the EPA, who came to the agency as Carter administration appointees, or who came at the call of the Carter reformers to fill career posts, were strongly committed to environmental policy reform. They were also strongly committed to certain ideas about the appropriate vehicles for reform, vehicles built largely on incentive schemes derived from the economist's interpretation of the pollution problem. Perhaps most strongly, however, the EPA reformers were committed to organizational changes they saw as necessary to the success of the reform ideas they sought to implement.

RRS Chief Michael Levin has concluded from his experience with implementing the bubble policy, for example, that "substantive reform . . . *must be backed by organizational change.* Reorganization for its own sake is an exercise in turf-building. But limited organizational change can send strong signals to the agency and outside constituents that the reform effort is serious, and place reformers in decision-making centers that require other actors to respond" (Levin 1980: 89, 91–92, emphasis in original).

In chapter 5, I discussed what many members of EPA's Regulatory Reform Staff saw as a critical problem in implementing emissions trading: the modification of the behavior of most actors in the air pollution regulatory system. That concern about behavior modification reflected the emphasis many members of the RRS placed on the need for organizational change to insure the success of emissions trading. The actions the RRS took with respect to "marketing" or selling the reforms, and transforming institutions, was part of this strategy. Many of the EPA reformers I interviewed discussed their commitment to organizational and institutional change. One charter member of the RRS, for example, laid out his own "champion theory" of policy and regulatory change. He argued that a "bureaucratic champion" who has an intellectual stake in a new idea must take up that idea and force it to permeate the system, overcoming inertia. In the case of air pollution control, that idea was emissions (or "controlled") trading and the bureaucratic champion was William Drayton.

In responding to questions about the roles they played in the development and implementation of emissions trading, two other members of the RRS expressed even more concretely the commitment to organizational change that was part of their strategy for regulatory reform. Their comments deserve quotation at length.

My own sense of mission was, I really thought economic incentives were a neat idea. I just really thought it was an idea whose time had long since come. The idea was to get this agency over its dead body to adopt that idea. . . . I went through the philosophical thing in terms of, "it's good for the environment, it's good for the economy," but the mission for me started under the Ford administration, through the Carter administration, and continues now [in the Reagan administration]. I would have been doing the same thing were I in the Department of Transportation, or OSHA, or whatever. It is the sense of mission that comes of forcing the agency to adopt a change which I thought was an innovation.

I always viewed my role as changing the fundamental way EPA did business. And it wasn't limited to implementing the bubble policy. And that's why we've expanded these approaches to all these other media now. EPA's done lots of things well and it's done lots of things poorly. There's lots of room for improvement. And this is one of the fastest ways to improve the process, again from the bottom up rather than from the top down.

This same individual, in responding to a question about the kinds of objections to emissions trading raised by the air programs and enforcement staffs, stated, "There were a lot of specific technical concerns. Some of which were legitimate and were responded to, which they have to be, some of which were covers for the larger objection that they didn't like people messing with their turf. You always get a lot of that. That is what a change agent is in business to deal with."

Acknowledging the need for "bureaucratic champions" or "organizational change agents" to accomplish major policy reform was not limited to members of the Regulatory Reform Staff, of course. One of the top political managers in EPA's planning and management office explained the importance of linking regulatory reform and management.

The reason for putting the two together is that I think they're the same issue. In fact, my . . . personal intent at EPA was pursuing both those avenues simultaneously. You can't have a turned-on yet integrated organization without having some of these same sorts of innovations in management [as in regulation]. One of the chief prerequisites for getting the body of people working at EPA, any regulatory agency, to think in terms of alternative regulatory approaches is for them to be working in an environment that is not a pyramidal bureaucratic structure, rather itself uses these sorts of tools.

This EPA manager went on to explain that he and his associates essentially proposed a new management and decision-making structure for the agency. He noted that in order to get program managers in the agency—and eventually others such as environmental groups and individuals in Congress—to accept the new system, it was mandatory that any policy reforms they pushed for, such as the bubble, had to be a product of the proposed new system, and in development and implementation had to follow that new process carefully, even religiously.

Finally, an EPA official who held a career post in the EPA administrator's office during the tenure of both Douglas Costle and Anne Gorsuch Burford described the organizational, even systemic, reform that seemed to be the ultimate goal of the Carter reformers, in the personage of William Drayton.

I believe that what was driving Bill was pure intellectual conviction that this was a truly elegant approach—The Right Approach, with a capital "T" and a capital "R." Clearly command and control was an inherently inefficient mechanism, an inherently litigious mechanism, an inherently complicated mechanism, and that [by] working beyond [those] laws to an incentive-oriented approach we could sort of have a Golden Age where we could get totally beyond the confrontational relationship between environmental advocates and industry.

When Reform Strategies and Organizational Character Collide

The bureaucratic political battles fought over emissions trading involved both questions of technique and questions of philosophy. Both arenas of debate and disagreement reflect the potential for conflict inherent in the organizational structure of the EPA and the divergent professional ideologies imbedded within it. Two observations about the strategy for organizational change undertaken by EPA's regulatory reformers thus seem especially pertinent. First, the agency's experience with emissions trading strongly suggests that the factional organization of the EPA is inevitably problematic for agency managers in the long run, especially when they and their political superiors face irresistible demands for policy change. Second, the imperative for organizational change toward an expanded role for economic analysis, on which the strategy of the Carter reformers was built, put that strategy on a collision course with the dominant ethos of the agency predicated on legal reasoning and the need for vigorous enforcement.

Designing a pollution control agency with fundamental tensions woven into its organizational structure and professional ranks seemed a clear political necessity given the sharply contrasting policy preferences of the Nixon

White House and the Democratic Congress in 1970. The necessity seemed even clearer to William Ruckleshaus as he sought to fend off challenges to EPA autonomy from the Quality of Life Review with the help of economic analysis. Despite the potential for internal conflict, the Environmental Protection Agency has made substantial progress in cleaning up the nation's air and water, the core of its original policy mandate. The agency's successes reflect the power of the founding ethos to generate a sense of mission and cohesiveness among EPA personnel. Nevertheless, the agency has also suffered significant setbacks, policy reversals, and has sometimes been slow to respond creatively to the discovery of new environmental hazards.

The EPA operates in a perilous political environment, emotionally charged and intensely conflictual. Agency policy makers and program managers find themselves in a much more exposed position than might be the case with other agencies because the EPA is so much more clearly suspended between the executive and legislative branches. Hence the agency is much more likely to be buffeted by criticisms from both sides. Moreover, the structure of the EPA is purposely designed to generate tension and conflict among the agency's clientele. As a result the agency is weakest when confronted with demands for policy change because the factionalization of its professional character often blocks the unity and consensus on policy direction the agency needs to tread nimbly through successive political minefields.

The EPA's experience with emissions trading epitomizes the agency's difficulties in dealing with demands for policy reform. It seems safe to argue that the Carter administration strategy to centralize decision making with respect to social regulation, and to inject a greater regard for efficiency in regulatory policy making, was not sufficiently detailed to take into account the peculiar character of agencies that would be directly affected by the drive for reform, or to consider the obstacles the push for reform might encounter within individual agencies. The strategy was essentially predicated on unleashing the technocrats under the control of the White House, and those positioned within regulatory agencies, as the means for achieving regulatory reform. For the field commanders charged with implementing this strategy, the Draytons, the Levins, and others like them, however, policy reform also meant organizational reform. These individuals were interested in "changing fundamentally the way the agency did business" and changing the "behavior in the system." By attempting change, and to a considerable extent realizing change, to make EPA policy and organization more closely conform with the technocratic vision, the regulatory reformers posed a direct challenge to the dominant professional ideology in the agency. What resulted was not only interminable wrangling over technique, but considerable philosophical and ideological conflict that substantially slowed progress toward the basic goals of the reformers.

Marcus (1980b: 175–180) offers a detailed assessment of the advantages, such as the lack of coercion, and the disadvantages, such as the slowness of change, associated with divided authority in the design of an administrative agency. That is not my central concern in this study. My remaining task, rather, is to pinpoint some appropriate lessons about policy and administration one may draw from the impact the movement for regulatory reform has had on an administrative agency, and in turn, what can happen to major campaigns for policy reform when they confront the peculiar realities that thrive within administrative organizations.

BUREAUCRATIC POLITICS AND POLITICAL LEADERSHIP

Students of public administration and public policy have long recognized the obstacles elected officials face in attempting to control their administrative agents. The problems actually arise on two levels. First, the political branches—Congress and the presidency—face enormous challenges in attempting to keep a tight hold on the reins of an independent and politically powerful bureaucratic apparatus. Second, political managers within individual agencies seem able to influence the direction policy will take to only an insubstantial degree.

On the first level, for example, occasions for effective congressional oversight of the performance of administrative agencies are spotty at best. Congress has at its disposal numerous forms of direct and indirect control over agencies (Ripley and Franklin 1987: 73–84). Direct oversight mechanisms, including agency evaluations conducted by authorization and appropriations subcommittees, and investigations conducted by the government operations committees, exhibit substantial weaknesses, however. Direct monitoring and surveillance conducted by committees and subcommittees occurs only infrequently, and usually on an ad hoc basis. Members of Congress have few incentives to be well-informed because oversight activity offers few political benefits. The sheer volume of agency actions potentially subject to scrutiny would overwhelm an already heavily burdened legislative calendar. And oversight is often subject to debilitating squabbles over turf. Oversight therefore appears relatively ineffective as a means for controlling the behavior of administrative agencies (Dodd and Schott 1979; Ogul 1976, 1981; Rockman 1984).

The indirect, nonobvious forms of control Congress can employ may compensate for some of the weaknesses of direct surveillance. Congress can influence bureaucratic policy making through the confirmation process for presidential appointees, through independent sources of information on agency performance such as constituent groups and the media, and through control of agency purse strings (Weingast 1984). Nevertheless, the structure of the American system limits the effectiveness of even these informal mechanisms of control. The competition and conflict within and between the political branches, purposely designed into the system as a safeguard against tyranny, provides considerable opportunity for autonomous administrative action (Miller and Moe 1983).

Presidents too have an array of tools they can employ to control their nominal bureaucratic subordinates (Meier 1979: 146–151). The organizational powers of the president to effect policy control include presidential appointments to top agency management and policy posts, creative staffing—vesting control over programs in a loyal White House staff, and reorganization. Presidents also have substantial control over agency budgeting, and a president's power to persuade and set the tone for his administration can have significant effects on the behavior of agencies.

Despite these instruments of control, the president's powers to maintain command of policy making in the bureaucracy are remarkably limited. The president is a stranger to the bureaucracy and he is far removed from the day-to-day tasks of most cabinet departments and bureaus (Heclo 1977). The president's time on the scene is limited to eight years, while many career executives may serve for decades. The president's policy preferences may so sharply diverge from those of career managers and policy makers in agencies that he may face insurmountable hostility to his agenda (Aberbach and Rockman 1976), although the president may over time be able to reshape policy preferences in the bureaucracy by the judicious use of appointments of friendly or neutral career executives to key positions (Cole and Caputo 1979). Presidential appointees often "go native" and are co-opted by the agencies over which they ostensibly have control. The time the president has available for attending to control of bureaucratic policy-making behavior is limited and grows more so as the president and his staff increasingly direct their attention to foreign policy and international crises. The president is heavily dependent on the bureaucracy for information, providing an agency counterbalance to presidential controls. Finally, the president must compete with Congress in attempting to shape the actions of the bureaucracy. For a variety of reasons, many administrative agencies have developed much closer ties to Congress than to the president.

On the second level, that is, within individual agencies, political appointees must overcome an array of obstacles to maintain control of their organizations and influence policy decisions (see, for example, Kaufman 1981). Appointees find it extremely difficult to resist co-optation into the mindset, institutional folkways, and policy preferences of the agency they are expected to manage. Political executives also face a time problem, as many serve for less than one presidential term. Little can be done to redirect policy in an agency in such a short time. Many political executives, because of their brief tenures in office, may be regarded as at most mere nuisances by entrenched professionals in public agencies. As with the president, political appointees are heavily dependent on their career subordinates for information, giving career executives a significant power advantage. When the policy intentions of a new political manager differ markedly from the prevailing policy preferences of the professionals in an agency, the political executive is likely to face hostility from frontline program managers and careerists in policy-making positions. Finally, most political executives are of necessity concerned with organizational maintenance and protection of an agency in what may be a hostile political environment. When the political environment demands the constant attention of political executives to external maintenance needs, this offers career managers wide latitude in controlling what happens inside the agency, including how the decision-making apparatus works and what kinds of policies it produces (Wilson 1979b).

Values and Leadership

What can the political operative, who remains loyal to the president, do in the midst of the bureaucratic thicket to help the president realize his program? Political managers may be able to influence agency policy under some circumstances. David Stanley (1965) found, for example, that by taking immediate action toward clearly articulated goals concerning an agency's programs, a political appointee can affect program actions in an agency. Joseph Zentner (1972) concluded that bureaucrats respond to political pressure only if, among other things, they are convinced the pressures have presidential support (both Stanley and Zentner cited in Meier 1979: 147). Harold Seidman and Robert Gilmour expand on this conclusion. "Organizational behavior can be modified and redirected by substituting new program goals, redesigning administrative systems, altering standards for recruitment and promotion, reorganization, training, and indoctrination" (Seidman and Gilmour 1986: 172).

The Environmental Protection Agency's experience with emissions trading offers just such a lesson. In the face of countervailing forces inside the agency, especially a dominant professional ideology opposed to the reform ideas embodied in emissions trading, political leadership was effective in nudging the policy apparatus in a new direction. Seidman and Gilmour generalize the argument. "To be effective as a 'change-agent' takes . . . leadership, a profound knowledge of institutional mores and programs, and, above all, time" (Seidman and Gilmour 1986: 172).

The Carter administration's commitment to well-defined objectives for social regulation, centralization of decision making, and a much expanded role for economic analysis in the design of regulatory programs created the political environment that exerted steady pressure for reform on agencies like the EPA. Inside the EPA, William Drayton exercised his political leadership not only by tapping the pressure exerted by the larger movement for regulatory reform, but also by making effective use of, and augmenting, the staff in the EPA already committed to economic reasoning as the basis of regulatory decision making. As chapter 4 documents, notable policy and organizational changes resulted.

What Seidman and Gilmour speak of in terms of leadership and organizational change, and what Drayton and his associates set out to do and what they accomplished, at least to a limited extent, reflect some of the most fundamental conclusions about organizational leadership to come out of the study of private and public bureaucracies.[4] Chester Barnard, for example, wrote artfully of the importance of what he called "executive leadership." Barnard saw leadership as vital to the creation of "organization morality." "Leadership . . . ," Barnard states, "is the indispensable social essence that gives common meaning to common purpose, that creates the incentive that makes other incentives effective, that infuses the subjective aspect of countless decisions with consistency in a changing environment, that inspires the personal conviction that produces the vital cohesiveness without which cooperation is impossible" (Barnard 1938: 283).

Herbert Simon offers a formal structure for understanding the importance of leadership in bureaucratic organizations. To Simon, decision making is the critical component of organizational behavior because "the task of 'deciding' pervades the entire administrative organization quite as much as does the task of 'doing'—indeed, it is integrally tied up with the latter" (Simon 1976: 1). Furthermore, "decision premises" are the crucial components of decision making. Thus, organizational leaders can influence the behavior of their subordinates most effectively by shaping the decision premises on which organizational operatives make their decisions, which in turn are the preludes to organizational action. Simon goes on to argue that an organization's leaders need not predetermine all decision premises. Factual premises are much less important for control than values premises because

discretion over value premises has a different logical status from discretion over factual premises. The latter can always be evaluated as "right" or "wrong" in an objective, empirical sense. To the former, the terms "right" and "wrong" do not apply. Hence if only factual premises are left to the subordinate's discretion, there is, under the given circumstances, only one decision which he can "correctly" reach. On the other hand, if value premises are left to the subordinate's discretion, the "correctness" of a decision will depend upon the value premises he has selected, and there is no criterion of right or wrong which can be applied to his selection. (Simon 1976: 223–224)

In short, political leadership in a public agency means setting the value premises for decision making. Philip Selznick makes a similar argument. "The institutional leader . . . is primarily an expert in the promotion and protection of values" (Selznick 1957: 28, emphasis in original).

"Organization morality" and the "value premises" of decisions are clearly integral parts of what I have been calling an agency's organizational character or governing ethos. Therefore, political managers in public agencies must reshape in some way organizational character in order to influence the policy outcomes of decision-making processes in such organizations. That, it is clear, is what Drayton and his associates tried to do. EPA's reformers not only attempted to change the principles underlying EPA's core regulatory programs, the reformers also pushed to alter the organizational fundamentals on which the agency's programs were based. Drayton and his staff shared a sense of mission, a sense of teamwork and cooperation, and a sense of dedication to task that reflect qualities Barnard associates with executive leadership. Moreover, they sought to control decision premises by reorienting EPA's policies and organization toward the values espoused by their technocratic ideology, especially the value of efficiency, and thereby radically reform the regulatory systems within EPA's domain.

Organizational Change and Ideological Conflict

I believe the evidence is persuasive that the regulatory reform movement has made a lasting impact on the ways in which the Environmental Protection Agency goes about its business. In the hands of EPA's regulatory reformers, especially William Drayton and company, the fundamental ideas of the reform movement have etched their mark on EPA regulatory policy, organizational structure, and the internal decision-making processes of the agency. EPA's pollution program managers are now more sensitive to concerns about costs, about efficiency, about flexibility, and about the problems of centralized control versus decentralized decision making with respect to pollution abatement strategies. Economic incentive concepts, especially the notion of air or water pollution rights as commodities that can be bought and sold in controlled or limited markets, have gained a foothold not likely to be shaken.

Nevertheless, reform is far from complete. The efforts of the EPA reformers so far have fallen short of achieving many of the reform movement's goals. The final Emissions Trading Policy Statement (ETPS) took over four years to evolve from the interim ETPS. The Regulatory Reform Staff has experienced some retrenchment in its influence over policy and the Air Programs staff has regained some lost ground, as evidenced by the following statement from the final ETPS. "EPA . . . recognizes that without strict accounting practices and other safeguards, emission trades may cause potential environmental harm" (U.S. EPA 1986: 43814).

Furthermore, the efforts of the Regulatory Reform Staff to bring incentive ideas to water pollution control have barely gotten off the ground. The attempt to use economic incentives to solve the chlorofluorocarbons problem collapsed. EPA reformers have failed to convince Congress of the need to change the statutory basis of EPA's command-and-control approach to air pollution abatement so that the agency's attempts to use economic incentives, which may provide needed flexibility to confront new air pollution control problems, can be backed by legal authority. Finally, fewer changes

in regulatory procedures and program office operations than the reformers
seem to have been striving for have taken place.

One conclusion to be drawn from all this is that the efforts of political
leaders in administrative agencies to inject new values into an organization
so as to restructure and "recharacterize" the agency can only go so far.
More fundamental or sweeping changes probably require basic policy, that
is *legal*, changes, which can only be legitimated by the legislative branch.

To understand what happened with respect to the limited success of
regulatory reform in the case of the EPA—to see, that is, what effects
bureaucratic politics can have on a significant movement for policy reform—
it is best to return to the observations of Seidman and Gilmour, cited earlier.
One of the biggest problems for the Carter reformers in accomplishing their
objectives was that they ran out of time. The reform efforts only really
began to gather momentum in 1979 and that momentum began to reach
its peak when Jimmy Carter lost his bid for reelection. The reformers
continued to make progress up to the very last day of the Carter administration. But that progress came to an abrupt end with the change of
administrations, despite the best efforts of a career policy staff dedicated to
reform. For the Carter reformers, the Reagan administration created an
environment much less conducive to their brand of reform. The important
outside political pressure, especially from elements attached to the White
House, and the legitimacy it lent to the reform movement inside the EPA,
had to be rebuilt. The rebuilding process substantially slowed the development of emissions trading, and gave the opposition within the agency
time to refine its objections.

More important than the problem of a lack of time, however, reform-
minded executives and managers in the EPA failed to gain sufficiently
intimate knowledge of what Seidman and Gilmour call "organizational
mores." The reformers failed in this regard because the reform movement
essentially was built upon a single ideological vision, based in economics,
which painted a singular picture of the proper organization, function, and
interaction of social, economic, and political institutions relevant to regulatory policy. The reformers already in the agency, and those who came to
the agency with the Carter administration, wore ideological blinders which
prevented them from fully appreciating the historical roots of the agency's
structure and ways of conducting its business. The reformers failed to understand fully that the character of the agency, the nature of its policy
decision processes, and the ethos that pervaded the day-to-day functioning
of the agency grew out of a different professional ideology that would be
the source of opposition to policy reform not just because of clashes over
turf or disagreements about policy techniques, but also because the dominant agency ideology defined regulation, its function and purpose, and the
proper organization of social systems for achieving regulatory policy ob-

jectives in ways that differed significantly from the ideology of the reformers.

What followed were philosophical challenges and ideological conflict for
which the reformers were much less prepared than for bureaucratic infight-
ing over turf and endless debate about techniques. Hence the EPA's experience with emissions trading offers a valuable lesson for politicians and
administrators of all colors interested in policy reform. At some point any
battle for reform must be fought within the administrative agencies responsible for a particular policy area. The failure to comprehend fully the
sources of the bureaucratic character unique to those agencies may result
in clashing professional philosophies and ideological conflict within the
agencies that could derail a reform movement.

Such conflict may of course be inevitable if the policy intentions of reformers contrast sharply with the attitudes and policy preferences of the
dominant professionals in an agency. But under such circumstances, reform
is not out of the realm of possibility. Given time—a variable reformers may
not be able to control—and intimate knowledge of an organization's bureaucratic character—something reformers may be able to secure—reformers may be able to effect organizational alterations sufficient to transform
policy completely.

POLICY ANALYSIS IN THE SERVICE OF POLITICS

Most students of public policy and public administration consider the
attempt to use the Planning-Programming-Budgeting System (PPBS) in
nondefense program development to have been a magnificent failure. President Kennedy's secretary of defense, Robert McNamara, initiated PPBS
in the Defense Department in 1961 as the means to gain greater control of,
and obtain maximum return on, the enormous sums of money being invested in the nation's secruity. In 1965, President Johnson ordered the use
of PPBS in a broad range of domestic programs. The marriage of PPBS
and domestic programs seemed doomed from the start. Francis Rourke
offers an enumeration of the irreconcilable differences between PPBS and
many government programs.

The troubles PPBS encountered are typical of the difficulties that confront all efforts
to apply the magic of managerial science to public administration. . . . [D]ifficulties
confront efforts to apply quantitative methods to domestic programs. Hard facts
on which measures of achievement can be based are hard to come by. . . . The task
of measuring the costs of a course of action can also be extraordinarily difficult,
especially because it is usually necessary to bring nonmonetary costs within the
sphere of calculation. Moreover, calculations of future costs and benefits depend on
methods of forecasting that are as yet far from perfect. (Rourke 1984: 172–173)

The successors to PPBS, including management by objectives, zero-based budgeting, and more informal attempts to bring systematic analysis and evaluation to policy development, have suffered similar fates. Yet all of these efforts have left a lasting organizational legacy. Although efforts to bring systematic thinking to the actions of government in a single, all-encompassing format have not succeeded, the commitment to policy analysis and the political necessity of having analytic capabilities within most administrative agencies has steadily increased since the introduction of PPBS.

Scattered throughout the bureaucracy, in departments, agencies, and bureaus, are policy planning and analysis staffs, of varying sizes and influence, working to apply systematic methods to the development and evaluation of government programs. Most of these units are staffed and managed by individuals trained in economics or in the principles of economic analysis as those principles have been integrated into, and have come to dominate, policy analysis as a distinct academic and professional discipline. Even Congress has an analysis arm of its own, in the form of a transformed General Accounting Office (see Walker 1986) to compete with the analytic capabilities of the bureaucracy.

The Office of Planning and Management in the EPA is an example of the organizational legacy of the drive to bring systematic analysis and program planning to government. OPM and its sister units with "crosscutting" responsibilities in other agencies continue to operate with the objective of bringing synoptic rationality to program planning and implementation and greater efficiency to the design and operation of government programs. The case of emissions trading and the EPA suggests, however, that analysis units in administrative agencies may serve another purpose: politicians can use planning and analysis offices as instruments for policy reform. In pursuit of Jimmy Carter's agenda for regulatory reform, William Drayton used EPA's Office of Planning and Management, which he headed, as the principal tool both for his attempt to transform EPA management and decision-making practices and for his efforts to reform the agency's core pollution control programs by introducing economic incentive ideas.

What happened in the EPA is not an isolated case.[5] Robert Bell tells a similar story regarding the Department of Housing and Urban Development (HUD) and its housing assistance programs. Bell notes that unlike many departments and agencies, "HUD was not strongly influenced, at least initially, by [the] trend toward comprehensive policy analysis and larger analytic efforts" (Bell 1985: 186). HUD had multiple policy analysis staffs scattered throughout the department, attached to program offices. These units were small and fairly narrow in their interests and impacts. In the wake of Richard Nixon's battles with Congress over his moratorium on subsidized housing and other HUD programs, and the president's impoundment of public housing appropriations, however, James T. Lynn came to HUD as its new secretary, replacing George Romney. Lynn was determined to use the department's policy analysts as his shock troops for transforming HUD and its housing and community development programs to coincide with President Nixon's reform agenda.

In 1973 Lynn merged the offices of the assistant secretary for research and technology and the deputy undersecretary for policy analysis and program evaluation to create an assistant secretary for policy development and research. Bell recounts Lynn's goals and actions in ordering this organizational restructuring.

Lynn's chief objectives were a massive reexamination of the federal role in solving America's housing problem and the passage of block grant legislation to replace the categorical community development programs. To achieve them, he promptly took steps to strengthen the center of the department and assert secretarial control. To head [the] newly amalgamated policy development and research unit and supervise the housing study, Lynn recruited economist Michael Moskow, . . . and gave him an expanded staff. Moskow, in turn, surrounded himself with economists and former academics . . . [who] saw themselves as bringing greater sophistication to HUD [policy] deliberations. (Bell 1985: 199–200)

Lynn was convinced that organizational changes and the use of policy analysis capabilities were the keys to realizing the objectives he sought. He regarded his internal departmental changes as quite successful. "By the end of 1974, in Lynn's view, 'HUD had one of the strongest policy shops in government.' Whether or not this high opinion of PDR [policy development and research] and its staff was justified, it indicates Lynn's confidence in the organization built during his tenure" (Bell 1985: 200). Lynn's organizational maneuvers were at least partially successful in policy terms as well. HUD's categorical programs were folded into the community development block grant program, enacted by Congress in 1974. The 1974 Housing and Community Development Act also included HUD's proposal for a new housing subsidy program, Section 8, intended to replace the housing assistance programs suspended earlier. However, Congress altered substantially the new construction component of the program from what HUD proposed, and some older subsidized housing programs were revived to address fears about the inadequacies of Section 8.

In detailing the accomplishments of James Lynn during his tenure as HUD secretary, Bell concludes that although Lynn succeeded in achieving his objectives in a limited sense, in broader terms, he failed. "If ever a HUD secretary had an opportunity to set forth a coherent rationale for subsidized housing policy, it was Lynn, and yet he ultimately failed to do so" (Bell 1985: 198). Much the same assessment might be made about the efforts of the regulatory reformers in the EPA. A valuable lesson from both these cases of failure in the midst of success, regarding the uses of analysis, deserves consideration. At a time when policy analysts are searching for an identity for their discipline separate from the dominant social sciences (see, for example, Paris and Reynolds 1984; also see Bozeman 1986), and when academic and practicing policy analysts continue to find too many instances where authoritative decision makers refuse to take analysis seriously, analysts and decision makers alike should pay heed to the manner in which analysis is often used. Despite the best efforts of some of the brightest policy scholars to make policy analysis an objective science, it is still easily molded to fit particular political views of the world.[6] Hence reform-minded politicians, whatever their station and whatever their ideological inclinations, have found and will continue to find policy analysis and the people who practice it useful instruments for pursuing reform objectives. Moreover, the power of analysis will continue to entice practitioners to become not just objective analysts, but policy advocates as well.

CONCLUDING OBSERVATIONS

Returning to some of the questions that energized my research into the politics surrounding EPA's development of emissions trading, what broad, if tentative, conclusions can one draw from this case of policy reform in an administrative agency? From the standpoint of organizational change, nothing in this study contradicts the widely accepted conclusion that bureaucratic organizations are extremely difficult entities in which to effect change. Similar to the conclusions Donald Warwick (1975: 197–199) reaches in his research on the State Department, the story of emissions trading in the EPA suggests that both external and internal factors play a role in influencing the success or failure of attempts at organizational change.

In the EPA's case, the external factors were less the agency's political environment defined in terms of other agencies and Congress, that is, its power setting, as Warwick refers to it, and more the EPA's political environment as defined by a broad political movement, and the commitment of a president and his political appointees to reform predicated on a specific set of ideas. The internal factors influencing the possibilities for change in the EPA associated with regulatory reform are closer to what Warwick concludes about the State Department. "[O]ur research provides unmistakable evidence that even the best-intentioned change program may be paralyzed by internal conflicts and cleavages" (Warwick 1975: 199). Here the EPA case points out that one important source of internal conflict and cleavage may be professionally based ideological differences between reformers and those opposed to reform.

As a case study of organizational change, however, I believe this examination of regulatory reform in the EPA stands apart from other studies in one important dimension. In most instances, organizational change is undertaken as an end in itself. Bureaucracy is widely regarded as an insidious, if necessary, evil that requires frequent reform to avoid its most deleterious effects. Hence organizational change must be pursued because it is inherently good, whereas the lack of change in a bureaucratic organization is inherently bad. In turn, organizational change should be studied to understand better what obstacles exist to change, and what changes make organizations better. Warwick (1975) and Thompson (1978) are superb examples of this kind of research on organizational change, or the lack of change.

The case of the EPA and emissions trading is not an example of organizational change as an end in itself, however. Rather, it is an example of a serious attempt at organizational change as the means to a larger goal: policy reform. Robert Bell's study of HUD and federally subsidized housing policy may be similarly characterized. Policy reformers employing an organizational change strategy as the means to reform may or may not face the same pitfalls as organizational reformers bent on organizational change for its own sake. The success of policy reformers may depend on how well they are able to limit the extent of the organizational changes they seek, as counseled by Michael Levin, and on how effective they are at keeping their opponents' attention focused away from the organizational changes and focused on the policy changes, where the merits of the issue may favor the reformers.

Clearly, however, policy reformers will want to pay close attention to what research on organizational change has revealed are the barriers to change in public bureaucracies. But the research focusing on change as an end in itself may not tell them everything they need to know. Organizational change as a means to policy reform may generate new roadblocks to change, as both the policy and the organizational reforms generate opposition of a very fundamental kind. As both my study and Bell's suggest, this opposition may be associated with professional differences and contrasting views of the world and the proper organization of society held by different groups of administrative policy makers as much as it is about battles over power, prestige, turf, status, and technique.

With respect to the politics of regulatory reform, two conclusions one can draw from this case study seem especially compelling. First, the prospects for the success of the current regulatory reform movement, concentrating as it does on new-style social regulation, remain problematic. This appears to be so, as the present case study bears out, because social regulation frequently represents the expression of fundamental public values and desires, such as the protection of public health and safety and the promotion of the public welfare. Attempts to reform social regulation thus face the prospect of being interpreted, rightly or wrongly, as attempts to change, or worse, undermine, such basic societal values. Under such circumstances, ideology becomes the guide to action and defines friends and enemies. In the face of ideological conflict, compromise that can aid in making progress toward policy reform is extremely difficult to achieve.

Steven Kelman has explored extensively the strategy advocates might use in pursuit of regulatory reform based on economic incentive ideas (see Kelman 1981: chapter 5). Kelman contends that the battle is over people's preferences and how to change them. He argues that the efficiency argument for incentives can be compelling, and he thus recommends that reformers concentrate their efforts on getting people to appreciate the efficiency advantages of incentives in areas such as environmental regulation. In other words, Kelman is arguing that reformers who advocate regulatory reform through the use of economic incentives should concentrate on increasing the weight of efficiency in preference orderings for public policy. Kelman points out that advocates of economic incentives are faced with the problem of getting people to make tradeoffs between the perceived costs of incentives along such value dimensions as equity, and the benefits of incentives along the value dimension of efficiency.

Regulatory reformers ought to consider Kelman's advice cautiously. Many of the arguments advanced by opponents of emissions trading, explored in chapters 5 and 6, questioned the efficiency of incentive schemes at a systemic level. That is, while opponents acknowledged that substantial gains in efficiency over commmand and control can be realized by *polluters* under the more flexible, decentralized pollution abatement system established under emissions trading, the efficiency of the regulatory system as a whole is much less impressive if one considers transition costs, operating costs, monitoring and enforcement costs, and transaction costs generated by the operation of a controlled pollution market.

Reform of social regulation using an economic model promoting a variety of incentive schemes thus may not be the most appropriate strategy. This is not to suggest that efficiency should not be a consideration in regulatory programs to protect public health, safety, and environmental quality. Other values, however, are likely to take precedence over efficiency. As Robert Levine (1972) has argued, economic incentives and other market-based policy instruments are most useful when stress is placed on allocation of resources. Levine observes that market-based arrangements do not do a good job of handing out rewards according to a socially desired pattern. Hence incentive schemes are more likely to be successful and useful where issues other than efficiency are not major concerns. Moreover, incentive schemes are more appropriate in policy areas where concerns over excess costs are widespread *and* where concerns over threats to the fundamentals of social existence—public health, welfare, and safety—are not pronounced.

Of course, as Levine points out, virtually all public programs raise problems of both allocative efficiency and distributive justice. The difficulty advocates of regulatory reform face then is matching the most appropriate mechanisms out of their tool box of approaches to the problems at hand. In the case of economic incentives, areas of regulation where less sensitive public values than public health and safety are at stake may be a better place to carry on the movement for regulatory reform. Regulation in transportation and commerce, exemplified by proposals to allocate airport landing rights and control airport noise levels through market-based techniques, may prove strategically more successful as targets for incentive-based regulatory reform (taking full account, of course, of the internal dynamics of the regulatory agencies involved). Some advocates of economic incentives, chastened by their experiences with reform of environmental regulation, are promoting the use of incentive-based regulation strictly in new areas of regulation (Gamse 1982). They argue that public problems not within the purview of strongly institutionalized regulatory systems, and which do not raise basic distributive questions, are more likely to be addressed successfully using economic incentives with the blessings of both legislators and program administrators.

Finally, the politics of regulatory reform, as seen through this case study of the Environmental Protection Agency, reveals important qualities about the American political system that are receiving increased attention from students of public policy. When professional ideologies serve as guides for evaluative judgments about public policy, as appears to be the case in particular in administrative agencies (in addition to the present case, see Bell 1985; Katzman 1980; Kelman 1981a), the fulcrum for policy debate shifts from interests to ideas. Ideologically driven policy deliberations tend to focus on alternative conceptions of the public interest and the broader public good and the most effective ways to achieve the public interest, given one's view of the world. What matters then are the policy alternatives themselves, that is, the ideas and how they fit into the professional ideology of the decision maker.[7]

Given the extensive influence over the shape of public policy exercised by administrative agencies, it is plausible to argue that to the extent an agency makes policy choices from among competing alternatives, those choices will be shaped significantly by the choices agency executives make as guided by ideological evaluations of the available alternatives. In turn, then, the policy process is increasingly focused on competition among policy alternatives, that is, on competition among ideas, and less on satisfying the claims of interest groups for special treatment.

I am not claiming that the traditional conception of American politics as the clash of diverse, competing interests is anachronistic. However, a variety of forces in the political system seem to be converging to diminish the legitimacy of special interest claims on public policy. Increasingly interest groups are finding that their special interests can only be served, at least partially, by promoting them as policy ideas that are consonant with widely accepted notions of the public interest.

With respect to administrative policy making in particular, the concept of clientele capture of regulatory agencies and the general notion that policy making in administrative agencies consists largely of some sort of tallying of the relative strengths of competing constituencies has always seemed somewhat out of kilter with the character of modern governmental bureaucracies. Public organizations are made up of highly trained, well-educated, skilled, and intelligent people. In most instances, they have been hired for their education, skills, and ideas about public problems. Organizations with these characteristics hardly seem the appropriate conduits for funneling the political ambitions of well-organized groups in society. Instead, the characteristics of the individuals employed in public bureaucracies would appear to guarantee that policy debate and decision making focuses heavily on ideas.

If the case of the EPA and emissions trading is any indication of the nature of regulatory politics in the 1980's, advocates of policy reform and innovation are likely to face strong philosophical and ideological opposition to the policy alternatives they seek to advance. The difficulties in overcoming the practical problems of applying their new schemes may pale in comparison with the barriers raised by intense ideological opposition. Reformers can expect to see their ideas succeed only if they can make a persuasive case on ideological and philosophical grounds, or can otherwise circumvent such objections. This is where the importance of political leadership comes fully into play. It will take not only time and luck to succeed with agendas for reform. It will also take intimate knowledge of the unique characteristics of the forges for policy ideas we call administrative agencies, and the skill to build political support for those ideas in the broader public arena.

NOTES

1. Ackerman and Hassler describe the New Deal model of regulation as based on "the affirmation of expertise" and its two institutional corollaries: "agency insulation from central political control" and agency insulation from "judicial oversight." Practical use of the model requires that "Congress should try to insulate the agency from other sources of power that might readily overwhelm its deepening understanding of its policy problem[s]. By making the agency independent from the executive and by endowing it with multiple commissioners, the New Deal makes it difficult for a momentary national impulse to affect agency policy" (Ackerman and Hassler 1981: 5–6). The authors note that in the attack on the New Deal model arising in the late 1960's and early 1970's, "expertise was seen as a myth concealing the inevitability of hard value choices, and agency insulation from political or judicial oversight as a screen concealing the capture of the agency by special interests" (Ackerman and Hassler 1981: 7; see the related discussion in Marcus 1980b: 20–21, 70–71). Some of the essential references on this topic are Herring (1936), Landis (1938), Huntington (1952), Bernstein (1955), Davis (1958, 1975, 1977), Friendly (1962), Stewart (1975), Freedman (1978), and Lowi (1979: 125–156).

2. A story related by a senior political executive who served during the Carter administration provides a lively, if indecorous, illustration of the intensity with

which many EPA staff were committed to the vigorous enforcement of pollution control laws.

I often had brown bag lunches and I invited speakers to come [talk to] my staff. We'd [just have] little talks about things that were interesting. My guys were all so smart that it was always a good experience for the speaker. So I asked Bill [Drayton] to come and talk about these concepts [economic incentives] very, very early on, and he did. One of the examples he used was what we came to call the "duck shit rule." It's a very minor regulation [put in place with] the first effluent limitations on nonpoint sources. One . . . was for poultry farms and the regulation actually said that the enforcement agency or inspector had to [go out to a farm]. The enforcer guy came and counted the number of ducks so that was the way they knew whether the duck shit in the effluent was over the limit. Of course it got to be a hassle. It was hilarious because the . . . duck farmer would say to the enforcer, "Go ahead and count the ducks." And he [the inspector] would say, "Well, where are they?" And the farmer would say, "Well gee, I don't know. They're out there somewhere." And there would be these terrible, terrible stories in the local papers about enforcement guys chasing around after these ducks. . . . Really dumb stuff. Bill gave that as an example [of the excesses of command and control] and I thought it was wonderful. [But] the guys in our water division just were furious. I mean . . . they got really worked up. They gave this justification where you had to do these things and you couldn't just let this stuff be uncontrolled. It went into a navigable stream. . . . I thought to myself . . . , this is really worse than anything I'd ever heard before. This is crazy. These people don't have any sense . . . [about how] to get out of what I called the silly areas. The sillies were always great, and troublesome to me as a political being.

3. Despite his background as a Justice Department attorney and his acute sensitivity to the political forces favoring vigorous legal remedies for environmental ills, William Ruckleshaus was not by any means unalterably opposed to efficiency considerations in making environmental policy decisions. He was in fact openly concerned about the need to take the economic costs that environmental regulations would impose into account. Ruckleshaus was, however, more comfortable with the use of the judicial system, rather than the market, as an instrument of social policy, and he recognized the political advantages of an agency ethos shaped by enforcement concerns. His readiness to consider further the costs and benefits of environmental regulation was more evident in his second tenure as EPA administrator in 1983 and 1984.

4. What William Ruckleshaus accomplished during his first tenure as EPA administrator, in helping to establish the agency's governing ethos and dominant professional ideology, is another case in point.

5. Martha Derthick and Paul Quirk (1985: 248–251) discuss in general terms the strategic use of analysis with respect to both organizational development and policy promotion.

6. The same can be said for much "scientific" analysis relevant to public policy. See, for example, Lowrance (1976).

7. The literature on the influence of ideas in the policy process is growing steadily. Some of the important works that have contributed to framing the research on this topic include Derthick and Quirk (1985: chapter 7), Kingdon (1984: chapter 6), Lowi (1979: Part I), Polsby (1984), Sundquist (1968), and Wilson (1979a, 1980: 393–394, 1986: chapter 22).

APPENDIX:
A NOTE ABOUT RESEARCH METHODS

Because information from the real world should instruct theory as well as validate it, case study research is most often regarded as the stepping stone or launch pad providing empirical grounding to formal theories about the way the political system works, which are then confirmed through more systematic empirical analysis. That exploratory or descriptive case studies of significant social and political phenomena are almost universally relegated to such a role has much to do with the limitations of case study research. Single case studies are usually limited in space and time, offering only a snapshot of the phenomena under study, although the same can also be said of much quantitative empirical research. More importantly, single case studies may illustrate arguments but they cannot legitimately be used to confirm hypotheses. Generalizations from the descriptive data derived through the investigation of a single case to the larger phenomena under scrutiny must be speculative at best. Yet the value of case study research in its role as prelude to more orderly theoretical development and empirical validation is substantial, as Nelson Polsby observes.

Case studies are a practical halfway house between arrant speculation and arid precision. On the one hand they provide empirical constraints that can guide speculation away from the embroidery of the genuinely idiosyncratic; on the other they can stimulate the production of ideas about how things are actually connected in the real world as a preliminary to more rigorous empirical demonstration. (Polsby 1984: 6)

Even with their limitations, case studies can stand on their own as valuable contributions to our understanding of the social and political world. Alfred Marcus's observations in this regard are instructive. "Most descriptive studies do not become the basis for further research, but stand alone on the basis of their merit and the interest of their subject matter" (Marcus 1980b:

xvi). My primary intention in undertaking this study of bureaucratic politics and regulatory reform was to explore and describe, and draw some tentative conclusions about, a larger set of phenomena concerning politics and public policy. Nevertheless, I believe it is appropriate to evaluate my research on the basis of its worth as a study of policy change and organizational politics, and for the scholarly interest of the questions it raises, as well as for its utility in instructing theory and helping to substantiate formal hypotheses.

DATA SOURCES

The public record and interviews served as the principal sources of data for this study of what happened when the movement for reform of social regulation collided head on with the organizational politics of the EPA. The analysis of documents from the public record served two purposes. First, the public documents provided an independent source of information on the history of legislative and administrative consideration of alternative regulatory forms, especially economic incentives. The public documents, in the form of the official records of congressional committee hearings and floor debates, and public filings from the dockets of EPA's notices of proposed rulemaking, also provided a large share of the information on the critical political issues raised by the reform movement's attempts to alter the form of air pollution regulation. The second purpose of the review of the public record was to inform the development of the questions used in the focused interviews and to provide an independent source of data to corroborate or reinforce the findings from the interviews.

Although I engaged in an extensive review of the public record, however, I intended the interviews with individuals who participated in, or closely observed, the development of emissions trading to provide the bulk of the original data for the study. I conducted a total of 65 interviews between June and October 1983. The 65 individuals I interviewed included many of the principal actors in what might best be described in Hugh Heclo's (1978) term as the "issue network" concerned with national air pollution control policy and the regulatory structure used to carry it out. The sample was drawn by initially contacting a small core group of decision makers, and then, through a process of respondents identifying other relevant contacts, what John Kingdon calls a "snowballing technique" (Kingdon 1984: 221), additional respondents were added to the sample. The total of 65 does not of course constitute a systematic sample of some larger population of decision makers. It does, however, include many of the individuals who exerted considerable influence over the direction taken in the development of emissions trading.

The 65 interviews included all but three EPA headquarters and technical field staff with formal decision-making responsibility for air pollution control policy and regulatory reform. In addition, EPA staff who participated in the decision-making process by invitation of those directly involved, including two individuals who served as full-time consultants to the agency, were interviewed, for a total of 28 EPA headquarters staff. An additional seven EPA field staff from the agency's Region V office (Chicago) were also interviewed because this EPA office, the largest of EPA's regional offices, was a highly visible part of the agency's implementation effort, and because a number of vociferous critics of emissions trading worked in this office. Six members of the congressional staff attached to the House and Senate committees with jurisdiction over environmental policy and EPA programs were also interviewed.

State pollution control agency staff are vital to the implementation and ongoing administration of EPA programs. I therefore included in the pool of 65 interviews nine state agency staff people from two states, Maryland and Wisconsin, because these two states have very active, very knowledgeable, highly professional staffs. The nine were chosen because they had special knowledge and experience with incentive schemes or because they had provided important input into EPA's decision-making process for emissions trading. Finally, I interviewed a total of 15 representatives from EPA's principal clientele, business/industry associations and environmental groups, who participated substantially in the extensive public review and comment that accompanied the development of emissions trading.

I structured all the interviews around a standard questionnaire. The questionnaire consisted of both closed and open-ended questions, providing the flexibility to depart from the standard format where the interview circumstances demanded it, although this happened only rarely. The design of the questionnaire with both closed and open-ended questions also served a number of other research objectives. The open-ended questions were meant to stimulate the individuals I interviewed to go beyond the confines of my questions in their comments and observations. In that way I could gather critical information in areas I had failed to anticipate in my choice of questions. I also sought to gather some hard data on the personal factors that strongly influence administrative policy decisions. Thus I included the closed questions in the questionnaire, although I put the data from these questions, and from the interviews as a whole, to only nonquantitative use in the book.

I designed the questionnaire for an interview of approximately one hour in length, and the average interview was completed in that amount of time. Overall, no interview took less than 30 minutes, and some extended beyond 90 minutes. I was successful in following the exact wording and order of the questions in the questionnaire in many instances, although it was sometimes necessary to vary question wording and order to fit the circumstances, and the flow of dialogue, of a particular interview. The complete interview questionnaire can be found at the end of this appendix.

DATA PREPARATION

I tape recorded all 65 interviews and had verbatim transcripts prepared from the tapes. This procedure takes extra time and effort to convince some individuals to submit to interviews, and it takes added resources for the preparation of the transcripts, but it is a step I strongly recommend to anyone undertaking interviews as a prime data source. The benefits of having unlimited access to the information provided by respondents far outweigh the rather insignificant costs. One can find a wealth of new data in the transcripts, invaluable especially to the preparation of a book-length manuscript, as was the case with this volume, even after three or four previous passes through the interviews as part of the data analysis.

Although I did the bulk of my analysis of the interviews simply by reading the transcripts, I also analyzed the data from the interviews in more systematic fashion by applying content analysis techniques to the interview transcripts. Using a coding scheme developed from the interview questionnaire, three coders worked independently to code data from the transcripts on: (1) the nature of the decision process associated with the development of emissions trading; (2) data on the critical issues in the debate over regulatory form that took place in the EPA; and (3) data on critical personal factors that influence the decisions of regulators. The coding team was trained in advance, provided simple step-by-step coding intructions, and disagreements over the coding of some items were resolved using procedures that would minimize post hoc adjustments. Although the quantitative data are not used, except indirectly, in the presentation of this case study, the methods I used to collect the data improved the overall organization of my research and the specific procedures I used for data analysis.

The design of this study, then, principally sought to begin the exploration of some important questions about regulation, about regulatory agencies, and about public policy generally that may not have been getting the attention from political scientists those questions deserved. Nevertheless, my study can also stand alone as an interesting tale of organizational politics and policy change inside a highly visible member of the federal executive establishment. In pursuit of the principal research objectives, I employed an approach balanced between qualitative and quantitative investigation, and formal and informal analysis. Most important of all was the opportunity to talk directly to the individuals involved. No other methods or data could equal the wealth of material I obtained.

INTERVIEW QUESTIONNAIRE

A. Personal and Professional Background
    To begin, I would like to ask you a few questions about your background and experience.

1. Please tell me about your education and professional training.
2. (If not clear from question 1) What was your undergraduate major? If you attended graduate school, what did you study?
3. How extensive has been your training in economics? For example, how many college economics courses or how much post-college training have you had?
4. In addition to those areas in which you hold degrees, what academic fields or other skills have you found particularly useful in dealing with environmental issues in your job?
5. (If not clear from question 1) Can you describe the positions you have held before the present one?
6. What, in particular, brought you to your present position?
7. (If an interest in environmental issues is not mentioned in response to question 6) Did you have a specific interest in environmental issues?
8. Can you recall how your interest in environmental issues developed?
9. Do you have a political party affiliation?
10. How would you describe yourself ideologically? Are you:
    a. strongly conservative
    b. moderately conservative
    c. middle-of-the-road
    d. moderately liberal
    e. strongly liberal
B. Environmental Regulation
   Next let me ask you some general questions concerning the development of methods for regulating pollution. As I believe you know, alternatives to the present system of what is called "command and control" regulation exist. For example, effluent and emission charges and taxes have been proposed. Another alternative involves the use of marketable or tradable pollution rights. For the sake of simplicity in my questions and our discussion, I'll focus on this latter alternative of marketable or tradable pollution rights.
11. How familiar would you say you were with the concept behind proposals for marketable or tradable pollution rights?
    a. very familiar
    b. familiar
    c. not very familiar
    d. not at all familiar (go to question 22)
12. Can you recall how you first learned about such proposals?
13. What kinds of material did you read regarding these proposals?
14. If you have discussed these proposals in conceptual terms with others, please describe the nature of these discussions, how extensive they were, and with whom they were held.
15. Have you ever written anything on these proposals? If so, please describe the kinds of material you have written.
16. Since you first heard a marketable rights approach advocated, has your opinion toward it changed at all? (PROBE: In what direction and why?)
17. In your own view, what are the advantages, if any, of marketable rights over strict command and control for pollution control? (PROBE with "policy effect" questions, if necessary.)

18. In your own view, what are the disadvantages, if any, of marketable rights over command and control? (PROBE with "policy effect" questions, if necessary.)

19. Although some form of tradable or marketable rights system has been advocated for nearly 20 years, it has only been in the past five or six years that action has been taken in support of such proposals, for example at EPA and in some state pollution control programs. In particular, Congress has shied away from such incentive systems for pollution control. Do you have any ideas why incentive-based pollution control systems have not gotten any further than they have until now? How have circumstances changed?

20. Who do you suspect are the major supporters of such proposals?

21. Who do you suspect are the major opponents?

Before discussing the EPA policies, I would like to ask you just a few questions of a philosophical nature about pollution control and environmental quality. (The ordering of questions 22 and 24 will be reversed for half the sample.)

22. One way of characterizing the pollution problem is to say that traditionally no one "owned" the air and water, and therefore no one wanted to take responsibility and incur the expense to prevent pollution or clean it up. Does that strike you as a good explanation for the pollution problem, or do you think there's more to it than that?

23. (If "more to it") What of importance is left out of this explanation?

24. Another way of characterizing the pollution problem is to say that traditionally most individuals and industries have been too socially irresponsible, and have not taken into account the effect of their actions on mankind and the planet. Does that strike you as a good explanation of the pollution problem, or do you think there is more to it than that?

25. (If "more to it") What of importance is left out of this explanation?

26. What criticisms, if any, would you make of the way we've gone about cleaning up the environment in the period since 1970?

27. If you had the authority and responsibility to draft what you would consider the ideal piece of air pollution control legislation, and the regulations that were to follow from it, what values would you seek to emphasize? Let me suggest some examples to spur your thinking:
    a. responsibility for the entire environment—the so-called "web of life"
    b. public health and welfare
    c. cost savings and cost effectiveness
    d. economic prosperity
    e. other values you believe deserve particular emphasis.

28. Why these values, in particular?

C. The EPA Policies

Now I'd like to focus directly on the EPA policies, that is, emission offsets and emissions trading, which includes the bubble policy and emissions banking.

29. How familiar would you say you were with the EPA regulatory reforms?
    a. very familiar
    b. familiar
    c. not very familiar
    d. not at all familiar (go to question 36)

30. Did you play an active role in supporting or opposing the development of the EPA regulatory reforms?
31. What was the nature of your role?
32. Can you describe some of the particular issues and concerns you raised during the development of the EPA policies and why you believed them to be important?
33. In an overall sense, what reasons do you believe explain the development of these policies by EPA?
34. In your own view, what are the advantages, if any, of these regulatory reforms over the strict command and control system? (PROBE with "policy effect" questions, if necessary.)
35. In your own view, what are the disadvantages, if any, of these policies over strict command and control? (PROBE with "policy effect" questions, if necessary.)

D. General Motives

I have two questions remaining that are somewhat redundant of items I've already asked you. These questions are intended to obtain specific measures to allow cross-comparisons.

36. This question again touches on the decision-making process for the policies. In your judgment, how important a role, if any, did the following considerations play in shaping the decisions that led to the development and implementation of the EPA regulatory reforms? Please use the following scale to respond to each consideration I read: 1 = great deal of importance; 2 = fair amount of importance; 3 = some importance; 4 = very little importance; 5 = no importance at all.
    a. knowledge and views of the staff in the various offices
    b. knowledge and views of superiors
    c. knowledge and views of colleagues and professionals outside the agency
    d. knowledge and views of environmental constituents
    e. knowledge and views of industry constituents
    f. general public opinion
    g. your own personal knowledge and convictions
37. Finally, given the views and concerns you have expressed in our discussion about the kind of regulatory system we should employ in controlling pollution, please briefly indicate how important each of the following considerations has been in determining your views. Please use the same scale as for the previous question.
    a. quality of the ambient environment
    b. public health and welfare
    c. cost, complexity, and burden of monitoring and enforcement
    d. the incentive for innovation in pollution control
    e. the nature of politics in getting a workable program
    f. changes in the political mood of the country and changes in the pressures on pollution control that have resulted
    g. concerns about stigmatizing polluting activities as wrong
    h. concerns about lessening the degree of social stigma attached to polluting activities
    i. concerns about buying and selling rights to pollute

   j. concerns that large, wealthy corporations will be able to pay and pollute
      more than others
   k. any other considerations?

      Record respondent's sex:

      Thank you for your patience and cooperation

E. Supplement: Policy Effect Questions
   1. Would such proposals (will these policies) cause environmental quality to
      be better or less well protected?
   2. Would such proposals (will these policies) decrease the costs of compliance
      with environmental laws?
   3. Would such proposals (will these policies) decentralize decisions so that the
      public would be less aware of what was going on?
   4. Would such proposals (will these policies) lead to a more equitable sharing
      of the costs of environmental clean-up?
   5. Would such proposals (will these policies) increase or decrease the pressures
      for environmental clean-up?
   6. Would such proposals (will these policies) increase the burden of compliance
      on industrial polluters?
   7. Would such proposals (will these policies) decrease the cost and complexity
      of monitoring compliance with environmental laws?

REFERENCES

BOOKS, ARTICLES, PAPERS, AND REPORTS

Aberbach, Joel D., and Bert A. Rockman. (1976). "Clashing Beliefs within the Executive Branch: The Nixon Administration Bureaucracy." *American Political Science Review* 70 (June): 456–468.

Ackerman, Bruce A., and William T. Hassler. (1981). *Clean Coal/Dirty Air*. New Haven: Yale University Press.

Anderson, Frederick R. et al. (1977). *Environmental Improvement through Economic Incentives*. Baltimore: Johns Hopkins University Press for Resources for the Future.

Barnard, Chester I. (1938). *The Functions of the Executive*. Cambridge, Mass.: Harvard University Press.

Baumol, William J., and Wallace E. Oates. (1979). *Economics, Environmental Policy, and the Quality of Life*. Englewood Cliffs, N.J.: Prentice-Hall.

Bell, Robert. (1985). *The Culture of Policy Deliberations*. New Brunswick, N.J.: Rutgers University Press.

Berstein, Marver H. (1955). *Regulating Business by Independent Commission*. Princeton: Princeton University Press.

Bonine, John E. (1975). "The Evolution of 'Technology Forcing' in the Clean Air Act." *Environmental Reporter* 6: 1–30.

Bozeman, Barry. (1986). "The Credibility of Policy Analysis: Between Method and Use." *Policy Studies Journal* 14 (June): 519–539.

Breyer, Stephen. (1982). *Regulation and Its Reform*. Cambridge, Mass.: Harvard University Press.

Buchanan, James M., and Gordon Tullock. (1975). "Polluters' Profits and Political Response: Direct Controls Versus Taxes." *American Economic Review* 65 (March): 139–147.

Cameron, James M. (1978). "Ideology and Policy Termination: Restructuring California's Mental Health System." *Public Policy* 26 (Fall): 533–570.

Cannon, Daniel W. (1977). "A Pollution Tax Won't Help Control Pollution." Reprinted in U.S. Congress, Congressional Research Service, Environment and Natural Resources Policy Division, *Pollution Taxes, Effluent Charges, and*

Other Alternatives for Pollution Control. Washington, D.C.: U.S. Government Printing Office.

Cole, Richard L., and David A. Caputo. (1979). "Presidential Control of the Senior Civil Service: Assessing the Strategies of the Nixon Years." *American Political Science Review* 73 (June): 399–413.

Dales, J. H. (1968). *Pollution, Property and Prices.* Toronto: University of Toronto Press.

Davis, Kenneth Culp. (1958). *Administrative Law Treatise.* St. Paul, Minn.: West.

————. (1975). *Administrative Law and Government,* 2d ed. St. Paul, Minn.: West.

————. (1977). *Discretionary Justice.* Urbana, Ill.: University of Illinois Press.

Derthick, Martha, and Paul J. Quirk. (1985). *The Politics of Deregulation.* Washington, D.C.: Brookings.

Dodd, Lawrence C., and Richard L. Schott. (1979). *Congress and the Administrative State.* New York: Wiley.

Drayton, William. (1980). "Economic Law Enforcement." *Harvard Environmental Law Review* 4 (1): 1–40.

Eads, George C., and Michael Fix. (1984). *Relief or Reform? Reagan's Regulatory Dilemma.* Washington, D.C.: Urban Institute Press.

Elkin, Stephen L., and Brian J. Cook. (1985). "The Public Life of Economic Incentives." *Policy Studies Journal* 13 (June): 797–813.

Fiorina, Morris P. (1982). "Legislative Choice of Regulatory Forms: Legal Process or Administrative Process?" *Public Choice* 39 (1): 33–66.

————. (1985). "Group Concentration and the Delegation of Legislative Authority," in Roger G. Noll, ed., *Regulatory Policy and the Social Sciences.* Berkeley: University of California Press.

————. (1986). "Legislator Uncertainty, Legislative Control, and the Delegation of Legislative Power." *Journal of Law, Economics, and Organization* 2 (Spring): 33–51.

Freedman, James O. (1975). "Crisis and Legitimacy in the Administrative Process." *Stanford Law Review* 27 (April): 1041–1076.

Freeman, A. Myrick III. (1978). "Air and Water Pollution Policy," in Paul R. Portney, ed., *Current Issues in U.S. Environmental Policy.* Baltimore: Johns Hopkins University Press.

Friendly, Henry J. (1962). *The Federal Administrative Agencies: The Need for Better Definition of Standards.* Cambridge, Mass.: Harvard University Press.

Gamse, Roy N. (1982). "Economic Incentives: Can They Replace or Supplement Direct Regulation?" in LeRoy Graymer and Frederick Thompson, eds., *Reforming Social Regulation: Alternative Public Policy Strategies.* Beverly Hills: Sage.

Graymer, LeRoy, and Frederick Thompson. (1982). "Introduction," in LeRoy Graymer and Frederick Thompson, eds, *Reforming Social Regulation: Alternative Public Policy Strategies.* Beverly Hills: Sage.

Hahn, Robert W., and Roger G. Noll. (1983). "Barriers to Implementing Tradable Air Pollution Permits: Problems of Regulatory Interactions." *Yale Journal on Regulation* 1 (1): 63–91.

Hayes, Michael T. (1978). "The Semi-Sovereign Pressure Groups: A Critique of Current Theory and an Alternative Typology." *Journal of Politics* 40 (February): 134–161.

Heclo, Hugh. (1977). *A Government of Strangers: Executive Politics in Washington.* Washington, D.C.: Brookings.

———. (1978). "Issue Networks and the Executive Establishment," in Anthony King, ed., *The New American Political System.* Washington, D.C.: American Enterprise Institute.

Herring, E. Pendleton. (1936). *Public Administration and the Public Interest.* New York: McGraw-Hill.

Huntington, Samuel P. (1952). "The Marasmus of the ICC." *Yale Law Journal* 61 (April): 467–509.

Jones, Charles O. (1975). *Clean Air: The Policies and Politics of Pollution Control.* Pittsburgh: University of Pittsburgh Press.

Katzman, Robert A. (1980). *Regulatory Bureaucracy.* Cambridge, Mass.: MIT Press.

Kaufman, Herbert. (1981). *The Administrative Behavior of Federal Bureau Chiefs.* Washington, D.C.: Brookings.

Kelman, Steven. (1980). "Occupational Safety and Health Administration," in James Q. Wilson, ed., *The Politics of Regulation.* New York: Basic Books.

———. (1981a). *Regulating Sweden, Regulating America.* Cambridge, Mass.: MIT Press.

———. (1981b). *What Price Incentives?* Boston: Auburn House.

Kingdon, John W. (1984). *Agendas, Alternatives, and Public Policies.* Boston: Little, Brown.

Kneese, Allen V., and Charles L. Schultze. (1975). *Pollution, Prices, and Public Policy.* Washington, D.C.: Brookings.

Landis, James M. (1938). *The Administrative Process.* New Haven: Yale University Press.

Lane, Leonard Lee. (1977). "The Politics of Pollution Taxes: New Opportunities." Reprinted in U.S. Congress, Congressional Research Service, Environment and Natural Resources Division. *Pollution Taxes, Effluent Charges, and Other Alternatives for Pollution Control.* Washington, D.C.: U.S. Government Printing Office.

Lave, Lester B., and Gilbert S. Omenn. (1981). *Clearing the Air: Reforming the Clean Air Act.* Washington, D.C.: Brookings.

Levin, Michael H. (1982). "Getting There: Implementing the 'Bubble' Policy," in Eugene Bardach and Robert A. Kagan, eds., *Social Regulation: Strategies for Reform.* San Francisco: Institute for Contemporary Studies.

Levine, Robert A. (1972). *Public Planning: Failure and Redirection.* New York: Basic Books.

Liroff, Richard A. (1980). *Air Pollution Offsets: Trading, Selling, and Banking.* Washington, D.C.: The Conservation Foundation.

———. (1986). *Reforming Air Pollution Regulation: The Toil and Trouble of EPA's Bubble.* Washington, D.C.: The Conservation Foundation.

Lowi, Theodore J. (1979). *The End of Liberalism,* 2d ed. New York: Norton.

Lowrence, William W. (1976). *Of Acceptable Risk: Science and the Determination of Safety.* San Francisco: William Kaufman.

McCubbins, Mathew D. (1982). "Rational Individual Behavior and Collective Irrationality: Regulatory Performance and the Theory of the Legislature." Unpublished Ph.D. diss., California Institute of Technology.

_____. (1985). "The Legislative Design of Regulatory Structure." *American Journal of Political Science* 29 (November): 721–748.

Majone, Giandomenico. (1975). "Standard Setting and the Theory of Institutional Choice: The Case of Pollution Control." *Policy and Politics* 4 (December): 35–51.

_____. (1976). "Choice among Policy Instruments for Pollution Control." *Policy Analysis* 2 (Fall): 589–613.

Marcus, Alfred A. (1980a). "Environmental Protection Agency," in James Q. Wilson, ed., *The Politics of Regulation*. New York: Basic Books.

_____. (1980b). *Promise and Performance: Choosing and Implementing an Environmental Policy*. Westport, Conn.: Greenwood Press.

_____. (1982). "Converting Thought to Action: The Use of Economic Incentives to Reduce Pollution," in Dean E. Mann, ed., *Environmental Policy Implementation: Planning and Management Options and Their Consequences*. Lexington, Mass.: Lexington Books.

Marcus, Alfred A., Paul Sommers, and Frederic A. Morris. (1982). "Alternative Arrangements for Cost-Effective Pollution Abatement: The Need for Implementation Analysis." *Policy Studies Review* 1 (February): 477–483.

Meier, Kenneth J. (1979). *Politics and the Bureaucracy: Policymaking in the Fourth Branch of Government*. North Scituate, Mass.: Duxbury Press.

_____. (1985). *Regulation: Politics, Bureaucracy, and Economics*. New York: St. Martin's Press.

Miller, Gary, and Terry Moe. (1983). "The Positive Theory of Hierarchies." Prepared for delivery at the 1983 Annual Meeting of the American Political Science Association, Chicago, September 1–4.

Mitnick, Barry M. (1980). *The Political Economy of Regulation: Creating, Designing, and Removing Regulatory Forms*. New York: Columbia University Press.

_____. (1982). "Incentive Systems for Environmental Regulation," in Dean E. Mann, ed., *Environmental Policy Implementation: Planning and Management Options and Their Consequences*. Lexington, Mass.: Lexington Books.

Moore, Thomas G. (1961). "The Purpose of Licensing." *Journal of Law and Economics* 4 (October): 93–117.

Morgan, Gareth. (1986). *Images of Organization*. Beverly Hills: Sage.

Ogul, Morris S. (1976). *Congress Oversees the Bureaucracy*. Pittsburgh: University of Pittsburgh Press.

_____. (1981). "Congressional Oversight: Structures and Incentives," in Lawrence C. Dodd and Bruce I. Oppenheimer, eds., *Congress Reconsidered*, 2d ed. Washington, D.C.: Congressional Quarterly Press.

Oppenheimer, Joe A., and Clifford S. Russell. (1983). "A Tempest in a Teapot: The Analysis and Evaluation of Environmental Groups Trading in Markets for Pollution Permits," in Erhard F. Joeres and Martin H. David, eds., *Buying a Better Environment: Cost-Effective Regulation through Permit Trading*. Madison, Wis.: University of Wisconsin Press.

Paris, David C., and James F. Reynolds. (1984). *The Logic of Policy Inquiry*. New York: Longman.

Perrow, Charles. (1986). *Complex Organizations: A Critical Essay*, 3d ed. New York: Random House.

Polsby, Nelson W. (1984). *Political Innovation in America*. New Haven: Yale University Press.

Posner, Richard A. (1974). "Theories of Economic Regulation." *Bell Journal of Management Science* 5 (Autumn): 335–358.

Quinn, Timothy H. (1983). "Distributive Consequences and Political Concerns: On the Design of Feasible Market Mechanisms for Environmental Control," in Erhard F. Joeres and Martin H. David, eds., *Buying a Better Environment: Cost-Effective Regulation through Permit Trading*. Madison, Wis.: University of Wisconsin Press.

Ripley, Randall B., and Grace A. Franklin. (1987). *Congress, the Bureaucracy, and Public Policy*, 4th ed. Chicago: Dorsey Press.

Ritts, Leslie Sue. (1982). "Summary of Comments: Emissions Trading Policy Statement & Technical Issues Document." Washington, D.C.: Environmental Law Institute.

Rockman, Bert A. (1984). "Legislative-Executive Relations and Legislative Oversight." *Legislative Studies Quarterly* 9 (August): 387–440.

Rose-Ackerman, Susan. (1973). "Effluent Charges: A Critique." *Canadian Journal of Economics* 6 (4): 512–528.

————. (1977). "Market Models for Water Pollution Control: Their Strengths and Weaknesses." *Public Policy* 25 (Summer): 383–406.

Rothenberg, Jerome. (1974). "The Physical Environment," in James W. McKie, ed., *Social Responsibility and the Business Predicament*. Washington, D.C.: Brookings.

Rourke, Francis E. (1984). *Bureaucracy, Politics, and Public Policy*, 3d ed. Boston: Little, Brown.

Sawyer, Kathy. (1985). "The Mess at the IRS." *Washington Post National Weekly Edition* (November 11): 6–7.

Sax, Joseph L. (1970). "The Public Trust Doctrine in Natural Resource Law: Effective Judicial Intervention." *Michigan Law Review* 68 (January): 471–560.

Schelling, Thomas C. (1983). "Prices as Regulatory Instruments," in Thomas C. Schelling, ed., *Incentives for Environmental Protection*. Cambridge, Mass.: MIT Press.

Schultze, Charles L. (1977). *The Public Use of Private Interest*. Washington, D.C.: Brookings.

Seidman, Harold, and Robert Gilmour. (1986). *Politics, Position, and Power*, 4th ed. New York: Oxford University Press.

Selznick, Philip. (1957). *Leadership in Administration*. Evanston, Ill.: Row, Peterson.

Shapiro, Michael, and Ellen Warhit. (1983). "Marketable Permits: The Case of Chlorofluorocarbons." *Natural Resources Journal* 23 (July): 577–591.

Simon, Herbert A. (1976). *Administrative Behavior*, 3d ed. New York: Free Press.

Stanley, David T. (1965). *Changing Administrations*. Washington, D.C.: Brookings.

Stewart, Richard B. (1975). "The Reformation of American Administrative Law." *Harvard Law Review* 88 (June): 1667–1681.

Stigler, George J. (1971). "The Theory of Economic Regulation." *Bell Journal of Economics and Management Science* 2 (Spring): 3–21.

Stone, Alan. (1982). *Regulation and Its Alternatives*. Washington, D.C.: Congressional Quarterly Press.

Sundquist, James L. (1968). *Politics and Policy: The Eisenhower, Kennedy, and Johnson Years*. Washington, D.C.: Brookings.

Thompson, James Clay. (1978). *Rolling Thunder: Understanding Policy and Program Failure*. Chapel Hill, N.C.: University of North Carolina Press.

Tietenberg, Thomas H. (1974). "The Design of Property Rights for Air Pollution Control." *Public Policy* 22 (Spring): 275–292.

———. (1985). *Emissions Trading: An Exercise in Reforming Pollution Policy*. Washington, D.C.: Resources for the Future.

Walker, Wallace Earl. (1986). *Changing Organizational Culture: Strategy, Structure, and Professionalism in the U.S. General Accounting Office*. Knoxville: University of Tennessee Press.

Warwick, Donald P. (1975). *A Theory of Public Bureaucracy*. Cambridge, Mass.: Harvard University Press.

Weingast, Barry R. (1984). "The Congressional-Bureaucratic System: A Principal-Agent Perspective." *Public Choice* 44 (1): 147–191.

Wenner, Lettie McSpadden. (1978). "Pollution Control: Implementation Alternatives." *Policy Analysis* 4 (Winter): 47–65.

White, Lawrence J. (1976). "Effluent Charges as a Faster Means of Achieving Pollution Abatement." *Public Policy* 24 (Winter): 111–125.

———. (1981). *Reforming Regulation: Processes and Problems*. Englewood Cliffs, N.J.: Prentice-Hall.

Willey, W. R. Z. (1982). "Some Caveats on Tradable Emissions Permits," in LeRoy Graymer and Frederick Thompson, eds., *Reforming Regulation: Alternative Public Policy Strategies*. Beverly Hills: Sage.

Wilson, James Q. (1973). *Political Organizations*. New York: Basic Books.

———. (1979a). "American Politics: Then and Now." *Commentary* 67 (February): 39–46.

———. (1979b). *The Investigators*. New York: Basic Books.

———. (1980). "The Politics of Regulation," in James Q. Wilson, ed., *The Politics of Regulation*. New York: Basic Books.

———. (1986). *American Government: Institutions and Policies*, 3d ed. Lexington, Mass.: D. C. Heath.

Wines, Michael. (1983). "Mission Accomplished, Bush Says of His Rules Task Force." *National Journal* 15 (34–35): 1749.

Zentner, Joseph L. (1972). "Presidential Transition and the Perpetuation of Programs." *Western Political Quarterly* 15 (March): 5–15.

PUBLIC DOCUMENTS

Irwin, William A., and Richard A. Liroff. (1974). "Economic Disincentives for Pollution Control: Legal, Administrative and Political Decisions." Office of Research and Development, U.S. Environmental Protection Agency, Washington, D.C.

Theiler, Donald F. (1982). Letter to Central Docket Section, U.S. Environmental Protection Agency from Director, Bureau of Air Management, Department of Natural Resources, State of Wisconsin, July 12, 1982.

U.S. Congress. Congressional Research Service. (1977). Environmental Policy Division. "A Legislative History of the Water Pollution Control Act Amendments of 1972." Reprinted in Congressional Research Service, Environment and Natural Resources Policy Division, *Pollution Taxes, Effluent Charges, and Other Alternatives for Pollution Control*. Washington, D.C.: U.S. Government Printing Office.

U.S. Congress. House. (1976). Committee on Interstate and Foreign Commerce. *Clean Air Act Amendments of 1976*. H. Rept. 94–1175 to accompany H.R. 10498, 94th Cong., 2d sess.

_____. (1977). Committee on Interstate and Foreign Commerce. *Clean Air Act Amendments of 1977*. H. Rept. 95–294 to accompany H.R. 6161, 95th Cong., lst sess.

_____. (1979). Committee on Interstate and Foreign Commerce. *Oversight— Clean Air Act Amendments of 1977*. *Hearings before the Subcommittee on Health and the Environment*. 96th Cong., lst sess.

_____. (1981). Committee on Energy and Commerce. *Clean Air Act*. *Hearings before the Subcommittee on Health and the Environment—Part 2*. 97th Cong., lst sess.

U.S. Congress. Joint Economic Committee. (1971). *Economic Analysis and the Efficiency of Government*. *Hearings before the Subcommittee on Economy in Government—Part 6*. 92d Cong., lst sess.

U.S. Congress. Senate. (1975). Committee on Public Works. *Implementation of the Clean Air Act*. *Hearings before the Subcommittee on Environmental Pollution*. 94th Cong., lst sess.

_____. (1976). Committee on Public Works. *Clean Air Amendments of 1976*. S. Rept. 94–717 to accompany S. 3219, 94th Cong., 2d sess.

_____. (1977a). Committee on Public Works. *Status of the Programs and Policies of the Environmental Protection Agency*. Hearings before the Subcommittee on Environmental Pollution. 95th Cong., lst sess.

_____. (1977b). Committee on Public Works. *Clean Air Amendments of 1977*. S. Rept. 95–127 to accompany S. 252, 95th Cong., lst sess.

_____. (1981). Committee on Environment and Public Works. *Clean Air Act Oversight—Part 1*. *Hearings before the Committee*. 97th Cong., 1st sess.

U.S. Council on Environmental Quality. (1979). *Environmental Quality—1979*. Washington, D.C.: U.S. Government Printing Office.

U.S. Environmental Protection Agency. (1974). "Standards of Performance for New Stationary Sources. Modification, Notification, and Reconstruction." *Federal Register* 39: 36916–36919.

_____. (1975). "Standards of Performance for New Stationary Sources. Modification, Notification, and Reconstruction." *Federal Register* 40: 58416–58420.

_____. (1976). "Requirements for Preparation, Adoption, and Submittal of Implementation Plans. Air Quality Standards; Interpretative Ruling." *Federal Register* 41: 55524–55530.

_____. (1978). "Report of the Bubble Concept Task Force." Revised: September 18, 1978.

_____. (1979a). "Requirements for Preparation, Adoption, and Submittal of Implementation Plans. Emission Offset Interpretative Ruling." *Federal Register* 44: 3274–3285.

_____. (1979b). "Air Pollution Control; Recommendation for Alternative Emission Reduction Options within State Implementation Plans." *Federal Register* 44: 3740-3744.

————. (1979c). "Air Pollution Control; Recommendation for Alternative Emission Reduction Options within State Implementation Plans." *Federal Register* 44: 71780-71788.

————. (1980a). "Ozone-Depleting Chlorofluorocarbons: Proposed Production Restriction." *Federal Register* 45: 66726-66733.

————. (1980b). "Air Pollution Control: Recommendation for Alternative Emission Reduction Options within State Implementation Plans; Proposed Revision to the New Jersey State Implementation Plan." *Federal Register* 45: 77459-77463.

————. (1981a). "Requirements for Preparation, Adoption, and Submittal of Implementation Plans; Approval and Promulgation of Implementation Plans." *Federal Register* 46: 16280-16282.

————. (1981b). "Approval and Promulgation of State Implementation Plans; State of New Jersey." *Federal Register* 46: 20551-20555.

————. (1981c). "Requirements for Preparation, Adoption and Submittal of Implementation Plans and Approval and Promulgation of Implementation Plans." *Federal Register* 46: 50766–50771.

————. (1982). "Emissions Trading Policy Statement; General Principles for Creation, Banking, and Use of Emission Reduction Credits." *Federal Register* 47: 15076–15086.

————. (1985). Office of Policy, Planning and Evaluation. "RRS Annual Report for CY–1984." May 31, 1985.

————. (1986). "Emissions Trading Policy Statement; General Principles for Creation, Banking and Use of Emission Reduction Credits; Final Policy Statement and Accompanying Technical Issues Document." *Federal Register* 51: 43814–43860.

INDEX

About the Author

BRIAN J. COOK is Assistant Professor of Government and International Relations at Clark University. His articles have appeared in the *Policy Studies Journal* and *The American Politics Quarterly*.